D0434929

Praise for *Strong Women Lift Each Other Up*

"'The personal is political' was a slogan of the women's movement in the 1960s and 70s. Molly has reinterpreted that concept for the twenty-first century, artfully weaving her personal experiences with structured curriculum to help women move past a competition and scarcity-based mentality. Molly demonstrates compellingly and practically how the 'ripple effect' of lifting up other women, even in small ways, can result in major shifts for us all."

— **Krista Scott-Dixon, PhD**
Head of Curriculum Development, Precision Nutrition

"Grounded in personal history, the empowering story of Girls Gone Strong, and an intersectional lens, Molly's book leads readers through the inner work necessary to empower themselves and the outer work necessary to empower other women. I'd recommend this book to any woman—and teenage girl!—wanting concrete recommendations on navigating mainstream diet and fitness culture, honoring their authentic selves, and 'lifting up' other women, for a more inclusive and equitable world."

— **Larissa M. Mercado-López, PhD**
Associate Professor of Women's, Gender,
and Sexuality Studies, CSU Fresno

"As a woman navigating a male-dominated field like Major League Baseball, I know how important the lessons in this book are. To move forward, create more opportunities for other women, and collectively elevate womankind, we must work together, using our unique skills and talents. This book shows you how to do that step-by-step. I wish I'd had this book in my early twenties."

— **Rachel Balkovec, New York Yankees,**
first woman hired as a full-time strength coach in MLB history,
first woman hired as a full-time hitting coach in MLB history

"Women *need* this book because if we want to create real change, #WomenSupportingWomen *must* be more than just a hashtag. Packed with inspiring stories, thought-provoking exercises, and practical ways women can support one another in the world, Molly's book goes far beyond just theory. If you've ever thought, 'I want to do something bigger, but I don't know what to do,' this book is your guide."

— **Colene Elridge, aka Coach Colene**
Creator of the EmpowHer Conference,
Author of *Monday Morning Pep Talks*

"This book is an inspirational, educational, and actionable guide to improving our own lives—and making the world around us a better place, with more opportunity for all women and girls. By the time you finish reading, you'll not only be inspired to make positive change, you'll know exactly how to do it."

— **Janae Marie Kroczaleski**
US Marine Corps,
powerlifting all-time world record holder

"With fierce passion, Molly Galbraith tells stirring stories of women who've made a big impact with ordinary but mighty actions and words; and with rare honesty, she vulnerably writes the things women only whisper to themselves. This book is a call to curiosity, to self-discovery, to awareness, to friendship, to courage, to imagination, to creation, to building bigger tables, and to making a difference in the lives of others by being you."

— **Reverend Angela Williams Gorrell, PhD**
Assistant Professor at Baylor University,
Author of *The Gravity of Joy: A Story of Being Lost and Found*

"We're at a critical time in history, where the perceptions of what women and young girls can become are shifting. Molly's book not only speaks to the possibilities and opportunities we can create for each other and the next generation of women and girls—she gives us simple, actionable ways to make it happen in our everyday lives."

— **Dr. Jessica Shepherd, OB/GYN, Women's Health**
Expert Founder of Sanctum Med + Wellness
Baylor University Medical Center

STRONG WOMEN *lift each other up*

MOLLY GALBRAITH

STORYTELLING WITH CAMILLE DEPUTTER

HARPER
HORIZON

Published by Harper Horizon, an imprint of HarperCollins Focus LLC.

Illustrations by Digital Brew
Text design and composition by Sarah Williamson
Cover design by Sarah Williamson, Grace Cline
Cover photo by Jeremy Kramer

ISBN 978-0-7852-3785-3 (eBook)
ISBN 978-0-7852-3908-6 (HC)

Library of Congress Control Number: 2020945787

Printed in the United States of America

21 22 23 24 25 LSC 10 9 8 7 6 5 4 3 2 1

To my mom, Susan, and my dad, Gatewood:
For loving each other, and for giving me life, love, and the best parts of yourselves.

To my sisters, Abby and Summer:
For your love, protection, and friendship. I wouldn't be who I am without you both.

To my grandmothers, Helen and Dollie:
For showing me the power of being a trailblazer and hell-raiser in your own ways.

To strong women everywhere:
For proving that together, we can change the world—one strong woman at a time.

Contents

Foreword

The year was 2015, and I was getting my ass kicked. I had just released my second book, *The Whole30,* and it became an instant *New York Times* bestseller. I was in the middle of a month-long book tour across the country with my Whole30 cofounder-turned-husband, and we were about to shoot our first episode with Dr. Oz. Dream come true, right?

Except while all of this was happening, we were smack in the middle of a divorce and business split.

It was a long time coming, but we hadn't told anyone yet, because we didn't want our publisher to worry about our ability to fulfill our contract. So when they booked us a hotel room for the tour, I quietly booked a second room. We rode to our events in total silence, but on stage we were the husband-and-wife show again. And when Dr. Oz asked us to walk up and down a midtown sidewalk holding hands for their B-roll, we clasped hands and painted on smiles.

Gross.

I felt like a fraud. I would go back to the hotel alone and in tears, wanting to celebrate but feeling exhausted from the performance. I was constantly on my guard, afraid someone would find out before we were ready to share. It was hands down the most stressful few months of my life.

When we returned home, we released one simple statement about our relationship and began divorce proceedings. I settled into single mom life while continuing to run the business alone. I wasn't sharing the real behind-the-scenes with anyone but my closest friends—it's hard to be a public figure and go through something this brutal. How much do I share? Is it anyone's business? Am I being inauthentic if I *don't* talk about it? I struggled to process the enormity of these changes happening all at once and where to find genuine support.

I'd been casually texting with Molly off and on after the book tour, and one day, in a moment of vulnerability, I shared that things were tougher than they looked on Instagram. I expressed fear and uncertainty around my business, and whether it could survive this split at such a critical juncture. Though we hadn't known each other long, Molly was a caring listener. It felt good to share my truth with someone, especially a woman who is also a successful entrepreneur.

A few days later, the mailman delivered a white USPS Priority Mail box, with Molly's name on the return label. I had forgotten that she'd asked for my address the last time we talked, so I certainly wasn't expecting to receive anything from her. I opened the box, not knowing what to expect. In a dozen years, I never could have guessed.

It was cupcakes.

A square plastic tray of gluten-free carrot cake cupcakes with cream cheese frosting. She *mailed me cupcakes*. Like, stuck them in a box, slapped on some postage, and sent them on their way. They showed up looking exactly as you might expect cupcakes to look had they been handled by two sorting facilities and multiple postal workers. They were, to be clear, a train wreck.

I ate every mangled, frosting-smeared one. (Not all at once, though.)

To this day they remain one of the most beloved presents I've been given.

Up until my late twenties, I didn't have many girlfriends. I always said it was because I got along with boys so much better, or that girls were too competitive or mean. Truthfully, it was because I was horrifically insecure, and it was easier to put other women down than look in the mirror and name the things I didn't like about myself. After many years of therapy, I finally started opening up to other women and went on to form wonderful groups of girlfriends both in New Hampshire, where I grew up, and Utah, where I live now.

Since meeting Molly in 2014, I've watched her model what it means to truly lift someone up. It wasn't about the cupcakes—it was about what they represented in that moment: *I'm here for you. I'll show up for you. I've got you.* Not because we were best friends or worked together, or she thought it would garner a return favor, but because that's just what you do when you notice a woman could use a hand. Her example has helped me continue to cultivate the kind of intimate, caring, loyal friendships I have today.

What Molly shares in this book is a bright light piercing through decades of rhetoric forced upon women by the patriarchy, the media, our workplaces, and, ultimately, each other. We are *not* competition—to the contrary, when we use our power for the good of us all, we are an unstoppable, unbreakable force. As

I have discovered by following Molly's example, when you lift up one woman, you lift up *all* women.

Through the lens of these pages, you'll begin to see your relationship to other women differently and start searching for opportunities in your everyday life to lift them up, whether friend or stranger. You'll find it easier to let others lift *you* up too. You'll accept the compliment, take the offer of help, and proudly let others toot your horn for you. Embracing the ideas Molly shares here will help all of us foster a new era of true sisterhood—where we use our privilege for good, leave no woman behind, and usher in an age of woman-to-woman camaraderie, support, and equality that I believe is long overdue.

Send the text. Offer to help. Mail the cupcakes. And most important, share the ideas and concepts in this book with the women you want to lift up. We are stronger together, and now is our moment.

—Melissa Urban, Whole30 CEO,
New York Times bestselling author

CHAPTER 1

How Lifting Women Up Changed My Life

The success of every woman should be the inspiration to another. We should raise each other up.

—SERENA WILLIAMS

CHAPTER 1

How Lifting Women Up Changed My Life

I distinctly remember the moment the girls turned on me.

I was on a field trip in eighth grade, rooming with a handful of other girls. A couple of the girls spread a rumor about me—that I had worn the same pair of underwear twice during the trip. As the rumor spread, they all started calling me "Two Wear."

"Hey, Molly," one of the girls called out. "What are you going *two* wear tomorrow?"

"Uhh . . . I don't know," I replied. "Maybe jeans, maybe a dress . . ."

"No, no. What are you going *two* wear?"

As I looked around at the group of giggling eighth graders, it became clear that I was the butt of a cruel inside joke.

A hot blush spread across my cheeks. I was embarrassed, confused, and hurt. These girls were supposed to be my friends. Why were they doing this to me?

The next day, I woke up feeling anxious and scared. I braced myself to be bullied again. But something else happened: a different girl became the target. You'd think I would've had some empathy for her—that I would have defended her or been on her side since I knew how it felt to be the target. Instead, I was so relieved the focus wasn't on me that I joined the group and made fun of the other girl.

Unfortunately, this was not an isolated incident. It was one of many encounters that taught me a damaging lesson: only so many girls can be accepted at one time, and in order to elevate yourself, you need to step on (or over) others.

The lesson took root. By 2001, I was seventeen years old and nose deep in gossip magazines, diet culture, and sorority life. As a college freshman,

I constantly compared myself to other women on campus. My stomach, my clothes, my grades, my life, you name it—they were all on the table for self-scrutiny.

Being nearly five feet eleven, I agonized about how much "bigger" I was than my friends. I never felt pretty enough, thin enough, smart enough, or good enough. My self-worth hinged on what other people thought of me. When boys thought I was cute, I was riding high, but when they liked my friend instead, I came crashing down. My self-esteem was a roller coaster. And while I loved my friends and cheered them on, I secretly felt like we were in competition with one another.

This sense of scarcity and competition showed up in other ways too. Take sorority life. During sorority rush, the "best" sororities had hundreds of women clamoring for a coveted spot. We were numerically ranked against one another and cut if we didn't measure up.

Similarly, the media I consumed was a constant barrage of "who wore it better," pitting female celebrities against one another. Magazines examined whose body parts were "best" and showed us readers how we could make our own abs/arms/butts/bellies look more like that.

Looking back, I can see that opportunities—for approval, acceptance, inclusion, or participation—often felt scarce. I viewed other women as my competition because there didn't seem to be enough to go around. Whether I was craving acceptance from the clique, inclusion into a team or sorority, or wishing for a "better" body, I couldn't help but see other women as an obstacle—or even a threat.

Then I met Taryn.

At nineteen I became totally hooked on fitness. To help me better recover from my workouts, I started seeing a massage therapist named Taryn Chula.

There was something different about Taryn. In addition to massage, she volunteered with a nonprofit organization that provides specialized care for women escaping human trafficking. She dedicated a huge part of her time to creating a better life for women. What's more, every single woman Taryn talked about—mutual friends, folks at the gym, fellow massage therapists who could be considered her "competition"—she spoke of with deep respect and affection.

She never said anything negative about another woman, and she got genuine joy from celebrating and supporting the women in her life.

When I look back on where the shift in my life and relationships started, I see Taryn. My conversations with her planted a seed within me about how I wanted to relate to other women.

I wish I could tell you that I became a champion of women right away. That one day I got up off the massage table with a commitment to support women and never looked back. But the truth is, at nineteen, I wasn't quite ready yet.

I believed "Strong women lift"—but something was missing.

Once I discovered fitness, I couldn't get enough of it. I worked out constantly and read every exercise and nutrition article and book I could get my hands on. I started dating a personal trainer and competitive bodybuilder, and by 2005 I was coaching clients too.

My newfound love of (or obsession with) fitness transformed me from a sedentary college student who got short of breath walking up a flight of stairs into a lean, lightly muscled fitness-magazine lookalike.

Men, women, friends, family—everyone wanted to know what my big secret was. The attention and affirmation were intoxicating.

While I was getting loads of positive attention, other women still felt like my competition. And in some ways they really were my competition: between 2006 and 2008 I competed in figure competitions, where I'd stand on stage in a tiny bikini to be—you guessed it—numerically ranked against other women and cut if I didn't measure up.

Fortunately, a series of events led me to see things differently.

In 2010 I cofounded a gym in Lexington, Kentucky, with a fellow coach and mentor of mine. My then business partner trained clients from all walks of life, but most of his clients were women, so I started training women too. Before that, it had never occurred to me to focus on helping women specifically. Yet the more time I spent helping women get strong, the more inspired I became.

Let me tell you: the first time a woman picks up a weight she doesn't think she can lift, the look on her face is priceless. My clients would jump up and down, clap, and hug me. Their initial gains unleashed a desire to get stronger and stronger. As soon as they set down the bar, they'd look at me wide-eyed and say, "Can we add weight? I think I can do more!"

It was awesome.

While my clients delighted in their inner and outer transformations, what they didn't know was that, by working with them, I was transforming too. Buried inside me, during all the years of comparison, jealousy, and competition, was a deep yearning to help women. Not just people. *Women*. I didn't have the language for it then, but I wanted to help them discover their own version of strength and show them what was possible for their lives and bodies.

I wasn't the only one with the desire to help women get stronger. In 2011, I got together with a group of fellow fitness professionals: Jen Comas, Alli McKee, Neghar Fonooni, Julia Anto, Marianne Kane, and Nia Shanks. We were all passionate about helping women get stronger, and we wanted to share that passion with other women. So together we created something called Girls Gone Strong (GGS).

Girls Gone Strong started as a Facebook page (and shortly thereafter a website) devoted to women's health and fitness, with a primary focus on strength training. The site included a by-women, for-women blog. Unlike other fitness media at the time, GGS encouraged women to get stronger physically, mentally, and emotionally. At the same time, we created a platform for female fitness experts to share their knowledge with other women.

Our idea took off. Industry leaders championed our work. Women from all over the world joined the GGS community. And a movement was born.

With growth comes change. As the movement grew, so did I. In 2012, I experienced heartbreaking loss, chronic illness, and personal struggles, which I expand on in more detail throughout this book.

I hit rock bottom. I was physically and emotionally exhausted, and I no longer had control over how my body felt, looked, or performed. I remember comparing myself to the other cofounders and feeling like I had no business being part of something called Girls Gone Strong.

I questioned who I was, where I belonged, and what I wanted for my life. Something was missing, yet I couldn't quite articulate it.

One day I stumbled across the phrase, "Strong women lift . . . each other up."

Something about it stood out to me. I read it again.

Strong women lift . . . each other up.

Up to that point, I believed I had been lifting women up by helping them lift weights. But at that moment I could feel my definition of "lifting women up" expanding. I thought to myself, *Wait a second . . . am I really lifting women up?*

After some deep introspection, I knew what I needed to do.

I could finally see that the years of obsessing about food and exercise, comparing my life and body to other women, and putting all my self-worth in external factors like what my body looked like, how much I could lift, or what other people thought of me was taking a toll on my physical and mental health. It was wasting my time, energy, and mental capacity and preventing me from becoming the person I wanted to be and doing the work I was put here to do.

I decided to make lifting other women up my mission—in work, and in life. Today, the "Strong women lift each other up" philosophy is woven throughout the fabric of the Girls Gone Strong movement—both in our community of over a million women in ninety countries and in our international GGS team. From employing and educating to featuring, collaborating with, and investing in them, we're dedicated to lifting up women all over the world.

To be clear: I'm not sharing this to brag. Nor am I suggesting I'm perfect, have it all figured out, or never have hard days, difficult relationships, or huge personal challenges. Believe me, I have these things in spades and have made countless mistakes over the years.

I'm sharing this because I want you to understand the power of lifting other women up. Supporting other women and being supported by them has changed every aspect of my life. It's helped me cultivate meaningful friendships, do work I love, feel good in my own skin, and live with a strong sense of purpose every day. It's funny, but after years of comparing and competing with other women, every good thing in my life has come from lifting women up. It's like a light turned on inside me that can never be turned off.

I've also witnessed how the concepts in this book can help us create not just better lives for ourselves but a better world for women and girls. Since the inception of GGS, more women have stepped into the weight room, discovered their inner and outer strength, and used that knowledge to help other women do the same.

Every time a woman lifts up another woman, it creates a powerful ripple effect. While there's still plenty of room for growth, in the fitness industry alone there are now many more opportunities for women: more women speaking at conferences, hosting events, opening gyms, collaborating on new ideas, creating products, being invited to speak on expert panels, and sharing their expertise online.

Whether it's in sports, government, business, academia, home life, or more, when women do the important work of lifting one another up, everything changes—for all of us. When women come together, collaborate with one another, have one another's backs, and support other women, we all win.

The women and girls of the world need you.

It's a really, really good thing you're reading this now. Not just because of the change you can make in your own life but because of the change you can make in the world.

We're at a unique period in modern history in which, globally, some women have more power, authority, and opportunity than ever. Yet we still have so much work to do. For example:

- Women are still paid less than men for doing the exact same work, and Black women and Women of Color are paid even less than white women.[1] What's more, there are critical, often invisible reasons why women don't even have the opportunity to do the same work as men, such as misogyny, racism, classism, homophobia, transphobia, ableism, and other factors.
- Women in the US are underrepresented in local and national government, in business, and in most places where important decisions are made.
- Globally, women spend twice the amount of time men do completing

unpaid domestic labor (e.g., cooking, cleaning, looking after children, caring for elderly parents, etc.).[2] In fact, in 2019, women around the globe performed enough unpaid domestic labor to equal $10.9 trillion dollars, more revenue than that generated by the fifty largest companies on the 2019 Fortune Global 500 list combined, including Walmart, Apple, and Amazon.[3] All this unpaid domestic labor means women have significantly less opportunity for self-care and personal and career development.

- Eighty-one percent of women in the United States experience harassment,[4] 27 percent of women in the US are survivors of sexual assault,[5] and 30 percent of women worldwide are survivors of intimate partner violence.[6] Every one of these stats is worse for Black and Indigenous women, trans women, women with fewer economic resources, and women with disabilities.

Let's face it: those stats are just the tip of the iceberg, and they are *unacceptable.*

That said, there is hope: *you* can make a real difference right now by choosing to lift women up, and each of us has the chance to do that, every day, in every area of our lives.

While we didn't necessarily choose scarcity mindset for ourselves (there are much bigger forces at play, which I'll unpack in coming chapters), we do have the power to change it.

For now, know this: other women are not your competition. When we buy into the belief that they are, we don't just hurt one another, we hurt ourselves.

Many women have told me they're tired of having surface-level relationships with other women. They want to stop looking over their shoulders, wondering if they can trust their female colleagues or peers. They want to stop comparing, judging, gossiping, feeling jealous, or worrying about what others think. They want to feel comfortable in their own skin. And more than anything else, they want to help create a better world with more opportunities for the next generation of women and girls.

I'm here to tell you this is possible.

I've spent the last seventeen years of my life as a coach helping women get from where they are to where they want to be. In this book I use that experience to walk you step-by-step through exactly what it takes to lift women up—starting with yourself.

I wrote this book to help you achieve strength, empowerment, connection, purpose, and the confidence to go after your dreams while lifting other women up along the way.

Change starts now. With this book—and with you.

CHAPTER 2

Laying the Foundation: Principles of Lifting Women Up

I considered my options. There were only two and they were essentially the same. I could go back in the direction I had come from, or I could go forward in the direction I intended to go.

—CHERYL STRAYED

CHAPTER 2

Laying the Foundation: Principles of Lifting Women Up

Throughout the last several years of my life and certainly while writing this book, I continually asked myself:

"What does 'lifting women up' actually look like in practice?"

The answer is not as straightforward as you might think. Let me explain.

I'm a blonde-haired, blue-eyed, white woman who grew up in Lexington, Kentucky. My thoughts, ideas, opinions, and perspectives have all been shaped by my lived experiences, and the same is true for you. Numerous factors, such as our geographic location, culture, gender identity, age, race, socioeconomic class, sexual orientation, and physical and mental abilities impact how we experience life and therefore how we go about lifting women up.

This concept is called "intersectionality"—a term coined in 1989 by the brilliant Black feminist legal scholar Dr. Kimberlé Crenshaw.[1]

But it isn't just our identity that shapes us. We're also shaped by things that happen to us (or don't happen to us) in our lives.

For example: Who did we spend a lot of time with as children? Who do we spend a lot of time with now? Did we finish high school? Go to college? If so, where? Were our caregivers loving and supportive? Were we bullied or discriminated against? Did our teachers believe in and encourage us? Are we survivors of physical or sexual abuse or violence? Does our family have a history of generational trauma from things like slavery or colonialism?

Each of our life circumstances is unique and special and affects how we go about doing the work of lifting women up.

Because of this, it's unlikely that you and I are going to have the exact same ideas about how to lift women up—or the exact same viewpoint on topics discussed in this book. And that's a really good thing! Because there isn't one right way to lift women up. It will look different for each of us.

By the end of this book, I'll help you narrow in on what lifting women up means for *you*. From there, I'll show how you can use your unique superpowers and personal values to create a better life for yourself—and a world with more opportunity for women and girls.

To do that, throughout this book I'll share my own stories as well as stories of other women, and while they may be different from yours, there are a few principles of lifting women up that apply broadly no matter who you are.

Principle #1: Believe You Are Worthy of Your Own Care

Have you ever heard the phrase: "You can't take care of others if you don't take care of yourself first"?

Maybe you've been encouraged to care for yourself because it will enable you to be a better wife, partner, mother, or friend. Sometimes this concept is positioned as "putting on your oxygen mask first," like when you're on an airplane and you're instructed to, in the event of an emergency, secure your own oxygen mask before assisting others. Many women use this concept as justification for working out, eating well, having hobbies, getting enough sleep, or engaging in self-care.

For many women, this may seem reasonable, but as I first learned from author and activist Erin Brown, its deeper message to women is that our self-care must be filtered through the lens of caring for others, while our own well-being often comes dead last.*

I'm here to tell you: you deserve your own care because you're a human with inherent worth.

You are worthy of your own care.

Let me say that again: you deserve your own care—separate from any

*Erin also was influential in my early adult experiences with feminism and social justice.

relationship with anyone else and separate from what that care may allow you to do for others.

While I understand the sentiment that taking care of ourselves allows us to better help others, this mindset could easily lead us to interpret the idea of lifting other women up as yet another thing we have to do for others while putting ourselves on the back burner.

That is not what lifting women up is about.

Having said that, we simply can't do our best for others while neglecting our own selves. Many women are held back in their lives by body image struggles, comparison, jealousy, fear, and doubt. These things not only hinder us from achieving our full potential—they prevent us from helping other women do the same.

For this reason, the first step to becoming a strong woman who lifts other women up is to do good for yourself, and the next few chapters help you address and overcome your own struggles before diving in to helping other women.

Principle #2: Embrace Small and Simple

In our GGS Coaching program for women, we see this situation time and again: clients enroll in our program expecting to receive a restrictive meal plan or complicated diet where they have to weigh, measure, and log all their food, yet we start them off with small behavior changes. For example, we may encourage them to put their fork down in between bites. Simple, right?

At first, this frustrates the heck out of them!

They want results fast, and what we ask them to do feels "too easy," so they're worried it can't possibly work. What they often don't realize is that long-term change requires *consistency*, so developing a sustainable strategy is a must.

Small and simple is a more effective way to make lasting change. Once again, this knowledge doesn't just come from my experience as a coach. It's rooted in change psychology. Evidence suggests that lasting change happens when you start small and stack good habits and practices on top of one another over time.[2] Once our clients do this, they achieve results they never dreamed possible. I've found the same applies to our topic of lifting other women up.

But here's the thing: small and simple can feel really weird at times. Especially if you're used to making broad, sweeping changes or if you've been told that minor efforts aren't enough to make a difference and you need to "go big or go home."

Embrace this motto: *small things add up*.

Even if you think one of the strategies in this book is too small to make a difference, do it anyway. I promise you, those small changes have the potential to make a real, lasting impact in your life and on the world. You'll soon learn how small acts can turn into huge (sometimes unexpected) ripple effects that create more opportunities for women.

Principle #3: Get Curious

As you read this book, you may hear voices in your head challenging what you're learning or doing. Those voices may take different forms. Here are a few to watch out for:

- the "I can't" voice
- the "I know this" voice
- the defensive voice

The "I Can't" Voice

The "I can't" voice says things like, "Sure, that's great for you, Molly, but I can't do this because . . ."

Or, "But if I did that, other people would think . . ."

Or, "I'm just not cut out for this kind of stuff."

Or (perhaps most commonly), "I don't have time for this!"

These thoughts sound perfectly justifiable. But they're tricking you into shutting down. When you decide something won't work for you, you eliminate the possibility of it working before you've even started.

The "I Know This" Voice

Sometimes that "I can't" voice gets really sneaky and says something like, "I already know this."

Or, "Yeah, yeah, I've heard that before."

Or even, "I tried that before, and it didn't work for me."

All of these reactions are a trap because your brain is giving you permission to dismiss or disengage from ideas.

In my many years of coaching, I've learned a lot about the difference between *knowing* and *doing*.

For example, you probably know the following habits promote better health:

- eating protein and vegetables with every meal
- drinking enough water throughout the day
- exercising thirty minutes a day, most days of the week
- cooking the majority of your meals at home
- avoiding excessive alcohol consumption

But how many of these do you absolutely nail, day in and day out, without fail?

Probably not all of them, right? That's because there's a difference between knowing and doing. And that's okay! We can't put everything we know into practice all the time. For lots of legitimate reasons, you don't engage in all of those health behaviors every day (maybe you don't even want to—and that's okay too).

The point is, I don't want you to dismiss the ideas in this book because you *think* you know them but aren't fully putting them into practice. You'll sell yourself short.

Recognize that you can keep moving forward, expanding, and improving if you approach the process with the right mindset.

The Defensive Voice

Some of the new ideas in this book may differ from your immediate personal experiences. At times you may not agree with what I have to say. You may even hear a voice in your head that wants to shut down or argue with what you're reading.

It may sound like, "Well, that's not *my* experience."

Or, "Easy for you to say, Molly. But that won't work for me and my situation."

Or, "That's not the case for me and my family."

As I mentioned above, our lived experiences are unique to us. However, we need to look beyond our own lived experiences and communities in order to achieve our fullest potential and lift women up in our lives. When you feel defensive or resistant (a normal reaction, by the way!), it's especially important to embrace an open mind and consider how other people's experiences differ from yours.

Curiosity: The Antidote to Each of the Voices Holding You Back

Curiosity is a key theme you'll hear about several times throughout this book, because it's an incredibly powerful tool for learning and growth.

Curiosity is your friend anytime you feel defensive, irritated, or resistant. Rather than denying your previous experiences or current struggles, curiosity invites you to see things with a fresh, open-minded perspective—to explore with a playful or experimental mindset. Curiosity refrains from judgment, moves us away from shame, and helps us create the space we need to give ourselves grace and compassion. As a result, curiosity can make just about anything more productive and positive, not to mention more fun!

If you hear any of the above voices, you can ask yourself questions like the following, which will engage your curiosity.

If you hear the "I can't" voice, ask:	» How can I make this work for me? » What could be a small way of trying or testing this idea out? » How can I experiment with this idea, just a little?

If you hear the "I know this" voice, ask:	» If I try this again, what might be different this time? » How well am I practicing this idea on a daily basis? What could I do a little more or a little better? » Is there a different way or a new angle I could use to apply this in my life?
If you hear the defensive voice, ask:	» Why is this upsetting me? » What beliefs or old narratives of mine is this challenging? » Even if I don't agree, is there a nugget of an idea or kernel of truth that I could learn here?

Fun fact about me: getting curious instead of defensive is one of my best skills . . . *unless* I'm in a fight with my partner, Casey.

Principle #4: Choose Your Own Adventure

As you read, you'll notice this book is packed with actions you can take in your own life. From here on out, you'll find a section at the end of each chapter called "Next Steps," with exercises to help you implement what you've learned. Some of these exercises will be short and simple; others may involve deeper reflection or observation.

How you approach these exercises is up to you. This is a go-at-your-own-pace adventure. If you want to do each of the exercises as they appear, that's great! But if you'd rather read the book uninterrupted and circle back later, that's cool too. At the end of the book you'll find a checklist to help you keep track of which ones you've done, and which ones you want to come back to.

No matter what: don't let yourself get stuck. If you can't do an exercise the moment you read it, or you're not sure how to answer a question, simply return to it later. You can progress at whatever pace suits you. The trick is to just keep going.

To get the full value of this book, I highly recommend you download our bonus Companion Resource Guide, so you can have it at your fingertips as you read.

You can find it here: www.MollyGalbraith.com/book-resources.

This Companion Resource Guide was designed to work interactively with the book, and inside, you'll find special content I created just for the readers of this book (including printable and fillable PDFs of all exercises in the book). You can pull your phone out and download this resource right now by going to the URL above.

As you read this book, I'll use the following icon to indicate when the information you're reading has additional or interactive information in the downloadable resource.

Find more here: www.MollyGalbraith.com/book-resources

Principle #5: Find Your Community

Want this journey to feel a little easier? Connecting with other like-minded people can help.

Ever heard the expression, "If you want to go quickly—go alone. If you want to go far, go together"? One of the most powerful ways you can set yourself up for success before you start this journey is to surround yourself with a supportive community.

Thousands of like-minded women want to help one another thrive. I know because I work with them every day in our GGS communities.

Connecting with like-minded women is beneficial because it helps you recognize that you're not alone on your journey, provides accountability and support, gives you a place to ask questions or get clarity, and allows you to learn from other's ideas and share your own. Plus, it lets you witness the "Strong women lift each other up" framework in action. To find all the ways you can become part of our community, download the Companion Resource Guide mentioned above.

I'm excited and grateful to be on this journey with you. Once you begin doing this work, you'll realize that "Strong women lift each other up" isn't just a motto. It's a way of being and doing and showing up that will help you live your happiest, most authentic, and most fulfilled life.

Let's do this.

CHAPTER 3

Disrupting Scarcity Mindset

Spend less time tearing yourself apart, worrying if you're good enough. You are good enough.

—REESE WITHERSPOON

CHAPTER 3

Disrupting Scarcity Mindset*

In 1983, the year before I was born, my father ran for commissioner of agriculture of the state of Kentucky. His platform? Legalizing industrial hemp and medical marijuana. Believe it or not, "legalize it" wasn't a popular stance in conservative Kentucky almost forty years ago.

My dad was an activist, constantly on the campaign trail, and he practiced law on the side. Being an unsuccessful politician didn't pay well. On top of that, my father was known for representing and defending folks pro bono. I remember when he drove across the state and slept in his car to help a woman win a custody battle over her abusive ex-husband, completely free of charge. He did stuff like that all the time.

We were financially insecure for most of my young life. Bills went unpaid, our utilities would sometimes get shut off, and I worried constantly about money.

I grew up feeling like there wasn't enough to go around.

Turns out, this feeling of not-enoughness is common among women. Not because our life circumstances are all the same but largely because women *still* do not have the same opportunities as men. And the opportunities that *do* exist are not divided fairly either—with great variances depending on factors like gender, race, class, sexual orientation, ability, and age.

Consider the workplace. McKinsey's "Women in the Workplace 2019" report pointed out that women are "underrepresented in every level," especially in management positions. The report suggested that this is partially due to a

---

* Throughout this chapter and occasionally in other chapters, I discuss my personal struggles with disordered eating and exercise behaviors and fat phobia. I know these are challenging topics for many folks, so please be aware, and be kind to yourself.

lack of promotions caused by "unfair, gendered assumptions about their future potential."[1]

As of May 2020, a record 7.4 percent of Fortune 500 CEOs are women—thirty-seven out of five hundred, which is up significantly from the last couple of years.[2] *Zero* of them are Women of Color. In fact, only two Black women have ever led a Fortune 500 company: Ursula Burns, who was CEO of Xerox from 2009 to 2016, and Mary Winston, who was the interim CEO of Bed Bath & Beyond from May 2019 to November 2019.[3] Across all industries, only 29 percent of senior managers are women.[4]

The numbers get even worse when you look at investments in women-founded companies. As of December 2019, only 2.8 percent of capital invested across the United States went to companies founded wholly by women.[5]

In the industry where I've built my career—health and fitness—things aren't so great either. Over the last fifteen years I've attended health and fitness conferences, I've noticed that—unless the conference is specifically geared toward women (which we've only started seeing in the last several years)—usually very few, if any, women speak at the event. On the rare occasions where women are represented, they typically make up fewer than 10 to 20 percent of all speakers, and almost none of those speakers are Black, Indigenous, or Women of Color. (They are also rarely over the age of fifty, in larger bodies, or people with disabilities.)

The public sphere suffers from similar underrepresentation. Women held fewer than 24 percent of US congressional seats in 2020,[6] and the global participation rate of women in national-level parliaments (equivalent to the US Congress) in 2019 was 24.5 percent.[7] As of 2020, women account for less than 11 percent of heads of government (i.e., prime minister, chancellor, president) globally.[8]

I could go on, but you get the idea. As women, we're facing fewer opportunities to speak at conferences, join important committees, get promoted to executive teams, get elected to public offices, and otherwise get seats at the "big tables."

The battleground of inclusion isn't just the boardrooms. It's also our bodies.

I was barely a teenager when I got the message that acceptance and inclusion depended heavily on what I looked like. And there was a very slim margin for what "look" was acceptable, desirable, or worthy.

For years, I was definitely not one of the cool kids.

The popular girls and boys didn't pay much attention to me, unless it was to occasionally call me "weird" or tease me for being flat chested. I remember showing up to gym class the first day of sixth grade and looking around the locker room in horror as I realized all the other girls had bras on, and I didn't. We had to change into our gym clothes, and they were going to see I wasn't wearing a bra. I pretended I had to go to the bathroom so I could change privately in the stall, hoping to spare myself the humiliation.

There were a lot of reasons I didn't fit in during middle school. Not having a lot of money and having a pro-cannabis father at the height of the "war on drugs" didn't help. But to me, it felt like my body was at the center of things, and approval and acceptance from the "cool" crowd was always just out of reach.

Then in 1997, the summer before high school, things started to change. My mom had been practicing law for a few years, and our family was a bit more financially secure. We had money for cooler clothes, for me to get my hair highlighted, and for my mom to pay an older, more experienced cheerleader to help me practice. I finally made the elusive cheerleading squad.

What's more, my body transformed. My breasts developed practically overnight.

Blonde highlights? Check. Big boobs? Check. Cheerleader? Check.

Suddenly, I was *in*.

I became friends with the cool girls on the cheerleading squad. Boys thought I was cute and no longer teased me for being flat chested. People who'd previously ignored or been unkind to me now paid attention to me, and some even wanted to be my friend. Looking back, it felt like that scene in the movie when the "nerdy" girl takes off her glasses and shakes her long hair out of a bun and suddenly the boys pay attention to her.

The message I took from this experience was clear: my body was the most important thing about me. It wasn't my personality or my smarts or my sense of humor that mattered most—it was how I looked. And I needed to look a *very* specific way in order to achieve the acceptance I craved.

Unfortunately, that experience wasn't a one-time thing. It was demonstrative of the very narrow beauty ideals we place on women in our society and how those ideals dictate which women are deemed acceptable, desirable, and worthy.

Want to see an example in action? Check out this powerful exercise inspired by Dr. Larissa M. Mercado-López, professor of women's studies at California State University, Fresno and curriculum contributor to our Girls Gone Strong coaching certifications.

The exercise is simple: google the phrase "successful woman."

I'll wait.

Done? Now, what do you see in common among these images?

The last time I did this exercise, nearly every single image was of a woman who:

- was young
- was white
- was thin
- would be considered "traditionally feminine"
- appeared to be cisgender (meaning the gender she identified with matched the sex she was assigned at birth)
- had no visible disabilities

To be clear, there was nothing wrong with the individual women who showed up as a result of this search. The problem was who *didn't* show up.

Black, Indigenous, and Women of Color (BIWOC for short), older women, women of different body shapes and sizes, women who present less traditionally feminine, LGBTQIA+ women, and women with visible disabilities are missing from our search results of what a "successful woman" looks like.

The message we get from this kind of limited representation is one of exclusion. It tells us that for women, success has a certain look. The subtext is that if you don't have that look, success is not for you.*

* Dr. Mercado-López says you can do this same exercise with "healthy woman" or "beautiful woman," with similar results. In fact, the original exercise she shared with me was to google "fit woman," but I've found this exercise to have broad application. Of

Moreover, the images we see (or don't see) affect how we see the world and how we see ourselves. While there are no current official figures, some experts estimate that we see four thousand to ten thousand images a day, and according to media scholar Jean Kilbourne, only 8 percent of an image's message is recognized by our conscious mind. This means 92 percent of the image's message is being processed subconsciously, shaping what we believe to be "right," and "true," and "normal."[9] As we repeatedly see the same images of women representing "success" or "health" or "beauty," we subconsciously start to believe that only women and girls who meet that criteria are indeed successful, healthy, beautiful, and worthy of opportunity. These beliefs are further reinforced when they mirror what we see in real life (e.g., fewer BIWOC, LGBTQIA+ women, and women with visible disabilities in leadership positions).

I could fill a whole other book on the subject of body image and how women's bodies are regulated, policed, and judged, but for now I'll just say this: our society's narrow definition of what's acceptable for how we look—and even more—the importance we place on women's appearance, is another way women experience fewer opportunities. Whether it's making the team, getting elected to local government, achieving a promotion, or gaining social approval, the message women receive is that we need to look a certain way—or we won't make the cut. Disturbingly, it seems that if we don't fit the mold, we have even less chance of getting what we need and want for ourselves.**

Phew! Okay, I've thrown a lot of head-shaking statistics at you. No doubt about it, big changes need to be made in the many systems that construct our society. It sucks, it's not right, and it's not fair.

And at the same time . . .

You have the potential to make meaningful, lasting, important change. You. Right now. In your life, just as it is.

How? Through an amazing phenomenon called the ripple effect.

---

course, it's not just the internet pumping out these ideals. Look at just about any form of media (movies, magazines, you name it) and you'll likely see a pretty narrow idea of what women "should" look like.

** Want to learn more about this? I suggest two books to start with: *The Body Is Not an Apology* by Sonya Renee Taylor, and *More Than a Body* by Dr. Lexie Kite and Dr. Lindsay Kite.

The Magic of the Ripple Effect

When you lift another woman up, it has an impact you can't always see. Lifting women up is infectious, and doing so can create a cycle of other women doing the same.

Let's say a female colleague of yours absolutely crushes it in a meeting, and you compliment her on how well-prepared she is and her willingness to speak her mind.

Maybe that one compliment gives her the confidence to:

- tell her boss she wants a raise
- apply for a promotion in her department
- see her value outside of just her appearance
- stick up for herself when her partner or mom is being overbearing
- quit her job and start the business she's been dreaming about for years

You've just made a bigger impact on her life than you could have anticipated.

But guess what? That's not all. Because *her actions* may in turn help other women. Perhaps:

- Taking her lead, more women in the office ask for a raise (helping close the wage gap in your company).
- By getting promoted, your colleague becomes a role model for younger women in your office or industry.
- By developing her inner confidence she inspires her friends and colleagues to do the same.
- Her daughter learns how to stick up for herself by watching her mom uphold her own boundaries.
- Other women see her chasing her dreams, and it inspires them to go after theirs.

And so on. The possibilities are endless.

This is the power of the ripple effect. Even a single positive action lifting another woman up creates a ripple effect that carries on far beyond the original act and has an impact that's difficult to measure. When you lift another woman up, you inspire others around you to do the same. And those opportunities continue to be passed on.

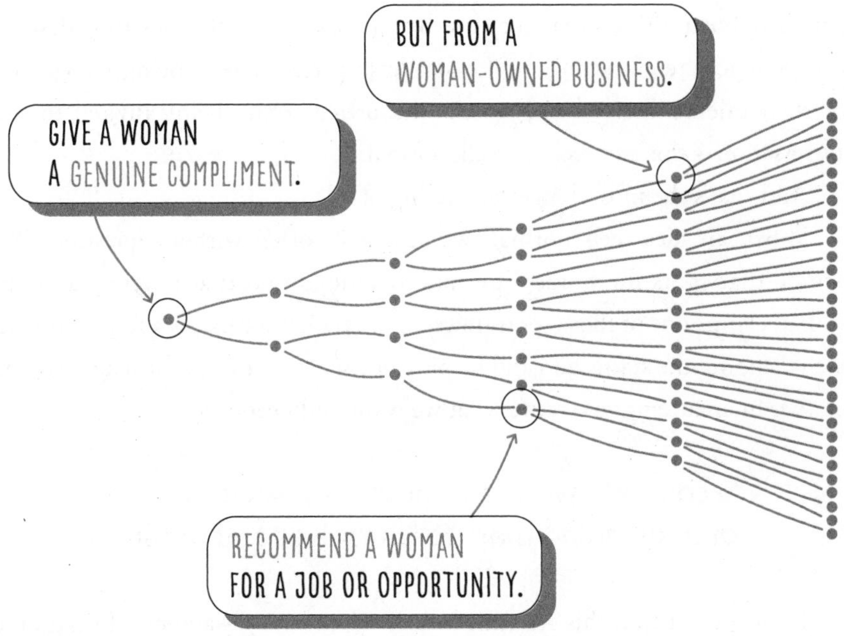

Think of the ripple effect like a candle. As James Keller said, "A candle loses nothing by lighting another candle." If we all take our candles and use them to light other women's candles, together we can create a wildfire that blazes a new trail for future generations of women and girls.

Look at the above illustration.* This is what happens when each woman decides to lift two other women up in her life and those women pay it forward.

If we're going to overcome the odds that a systemic lack of opportunity stacks against us, we must work together.

It won't be easy. It's going to take knowledge, skill, and strategy to get there,

* Inspired by an illustration Toby Morris (@xtotl) created for an article by Dr. Siouxsie Wiles (@siouxsiew) for the Spinoff: https://thespinoff.co.nz/media/04-09-2020/the-great-toby-morris-siouxsie-wiles-covid-19-omnibus/.

but most important of all, it's going to take you, me, and the women reading this book believing that we can make a difference by lifting other women up.

Because here's the thing: there absolutely can be equitable representation of women in executive positions, leadership positions, key political roles—you name it. But when we look around and see that fewer women are included or getting opportunities—that they are being passed over for jobs they deserve or experiences required to hold key leadership roles, aren't being recognized for their talents, aren't being voted into office, aren't being invited to the conversation—this can feel . . . well, normal.

And that's the most dangerous feeling of all.

When an idea feels normal, we accept it, often without question. We assume that spots for women are indeed limited and that anytime another woman claims one of those spots, fewer spots are left for us. As a result, instead of challenging the status quo and helping our sisters, we often turn against one another in an attempt to secure what we want and need.

We compete with one another for scraps instead of demanding more for ourselves and others.

In my experience, this systemic lack of opportunity—and belief that some women are more likely to get those opportunities—breeds feelings of scarcity and can lead to things like comparison, jealousy, body image struggles, and feeling less than. It can even translate into catty and competitive relationships with other women.

I call this scarcity mindset, and it's a huge obstacle we each need to overcome before we can lift other women up.

Scarcity Mindset Stands in Our Way

I'm pretty familiar with the feeling of scarcity.

As you now know, I grew up without much financial certainty. My parents divorced when I was very young, and shortly thereafter my mom (one of the most badass women I know) went back to law school at age thirty-seven as a single mother of three girls. During that time, my mom would take us to the grocery store, and she'd sit in our van and study while my sisters and I—at ages seven, ten, and twelve—would do the shopping. We'd have a pre-signed check with just enough money to buy food for the week. I often remember standing at the cash register, realizing we didn't have enough money, and having to decide what to put back.

I constantly worried there wouldn't be enough of what I wanted or needed. I had a continual feeling of not-enoughness, and I believed that if somebody else had some, there was less left for me because, in a lot of ways, that was true.

At the same time, I had a sense of dread and shame about having less. I hated school field trips, which most kids loved, because I couldn't stand the look on my mom's face when I had to ask her for five dollars. And I remember being upset in the fifth grade when my jeans got a hole in the knee. I only had one pair of jeans, and I thought if they had a hole in them, everyone would know I wore the same pair of jeans almost every day.

Money wasn't the only thing that felt scarce. Attention, approval, and inclusion felt scarce too. My father was well known in Kentucky when I was growing up. In fact, he was downright notorious for his progressive stance on industrial hemp and medical marijuana.

In 1994, when I was in middle school, he was campaigning for the 1995 gubernatorial race, and the media was positioning him as the "pothead" political candidate. While some people celebrated his now-legendary efforts (he was decades ahead of his time), most folks in our community weren't as forward thinking, and lots of people were judgmental and even cruel. Some kids weren't allowed to come over to my house, and others weren't allowed to be friends with me at all. I loved my dad, but during those days all I wanted was to fit in and be accepted and seen as "normal."

That's why I tried out for cheerleading on three different occasions, despite getting rejected each time (I finally made it on my fourth try). At my school the cheerleaders were considered pretty and popular, and I thought if I made the squad, I might be considered pretty and popular too. Every time I was rejected, it was so painful I cried my eyes out.[10]

I wanted so badly to be included and accepted that I was willing to be a bystander (or even participate) when other girls got bullied. And I *agonized* over my body and spent years trying to change it (more about that in a bit).

I bought into the idea that anytime another girl claimed a spot, there was one less spot available for me.

I wish I could go back and do things differently. I also wish I could go back and tell young Molly that she's good enough just as she is. But I can't. What I can do is pass along what I've learned to you and other women.

In my seventeen years as a coach, and through the work we do with women at Girls Gone Strong, I've seen that the very real lack of opportunity available for women causes them to struggle with scarcity mindset, just as the experiences I had early in my life entrenched scarcity mindset in me.

And I know this: when things are scarce, you feel like there's never enough to go around, whether it's acceptance, success, opportunity, money, or other resources—and you feel less inclined to help other people out (or lift women up).

If we're going to make the difference we're capable of making and truly live our best, strongest, and most impactful lives, we have to challenge this mindset.

And the place to start is with ourselves.

We Have to Fix Our Own Shit First

In order for you to become a strong woman who lifts other women up, you must first be willing to disrupt the ways scarcity mindset shows up in your life.

Just as "lifting women up" will be different for each of us based on our lived experiences, the ways scarcity mindset shows up for each of us will be different too. (You can use the "Next Steps" actions at the end of this chapter to help identify how it shows up for you.)

That said, for many women, scarcity mindset shows up in the form of body image issues.

Certainly this was the case for me. For years, an obsession with my body dominated my life. I discovered fitness and nutrition in college, and while this helped me feel better physically (for a while), I got caught up in diet culture. I was consumed by the idea that "fat" was bad, and "lean" was good—at any cost. I don't agree whatsoever with this perspective anymore. But that's how I thought at the time.

At age twenty-two, I did my first figure competition. Figure competitions are similar to bodybuilding, except your body isn't as lean and muscular as a bodybuilder's. However, you still stand on stage in a tiny bikini in front of a group of judges, who score and rank your body in comparison to the bodies of the other women on stage.

To compete, I had to get super lean. So I dieted for twelve to sixteen weeks, often eating less than nine hundred calories a day, and did two hours of cardio a day as well as strength training.

As soon as the competition ended, I couldn't control myself around food. I binged and gained fifteen to twenty pounds within a few weeks. The response from other people was dramatic. When I was lean, people showered me with praise. But now those same people said things like, "Whoa, what happened to you?" or "Are you still doing that working out thing?"

Their reactions made me desperate to "get my body back," and the only way I knew how to do this was to sign up for another competition. This became my pattern: get super lean, compete, rebound. I remained trapped in this vicious cycle for several years.

Then, after my final competition, I hit a wall. I had horrible fatigue, brain fog, and super wacky menstrual cycles. After a few months, I went to the doctor, who diagnosed me with Hashimoto's (an autoimmune thyroid disease), polycystic ovarian syndrome (known as PCOS), and adrenal dysfunction, which my doctor described as a "feedback loop issue between my brain and my adrenals."* For the first time in my adult life, I couldn't control the way my body looked and felt. All of my nutrition and exercise strategies no longer worked. I gained weight.

In turn, all the positive attention I'd received about my body seemed to

* I'd like to acknowledge that I was lucky to receive those accurate diagnoses so quickly. Many women with autoimmune diseases have told me they had to see multiple doctors over several years before getting an accurate diagnosis. I also was fortunate enough to have access to a great doctor and the ability to pay for a battery of tests, supplements, and medications, not covered by insurance—one of many ways my privilege has afforded me the support other women don't have.

evaporate overnight. Instead of receiving praise for my body, it felt like everyone couldn't believe how my body had changed and how much weight I'd gained.

I'd worried about my body my entire life and wrapped up my self-worth in what other people thought of my appearance. I'd hinged my identity on being the "super lean, fit girl." Suddenly, that affirmation and identity were ripped away from me. My body wasn't responding the way it had before, and I had to stop dieting and trying to control my body weight if I wanted a shot at getting healthy.

Desperate for some kind of assurance, I thought to myself, *Okay, if I can't be the really fit, lean girl, I'm going to be the really strong girl.*

I decided to compete in powerlifting. I mustered the little bit of energy I had each day and went to the gym to train for a powerlifting meet. Powerlifting is a sport where you compete in three different events: the barbell back squat, the barbell bench press, and the barbell deadlift. In each event, the goal is to see how much weight you can lift. The heavier, the better.

I competed in spring 2009 and had a great time at the meet. I set some personal records and got a lot of praise and support from other people for being strong. I walked away from the meet deciding that powerlifting was going to be "my thing."

For the next couple of years, I trained for powerlifting while working with my doctor to get my Hashimoto's, PCOS, and adrenal issues under control. Of course, I also was working with my cofounders to build Girls Gone Strong during this time. And by the beginning of 2012, I was starting to feel better.

And then my world came crashing down.

My dad died unexpectedly. I found out he was sick on a Saturday and he died that Tuesday night. Shortly after, I injured myself in the gym, kicking off two years of chronic back pain where I could hardly tie my shoes, much less work out like I had previously. Later that year, I left a six-year relationship, including the business and house we had together, and moved home with my mom.

At twenty-eight years old, it felt like everything in my life had fallen apart. As you can imagine, nutrition and exercise weren't my top priorities, and once again I gained weight.

That November I attended a Girls Gone Strong meetup with a couple of other GGS cofounders. I couldn't help but compare myself to them. They were deadlifting double their bodyweights and doing weighted pull-ups with twenty-five pounds, and there I was, lying on my back doing breathing exercises because I was in so much pain.

At one point during the meetup, I took a bathroom break. When I walked into the bathroom, I noticed the gym scale. I hadn't weighed myself for a while, so out of curiosity, I stepped on the scale. When I saw the number, I gasped. I was only 1.5 pounds lighter than I'd weighed almost nine years before, when I started my health and fitness journey. All those years restricting, obsessing, stressing, trying so hard to be lean and strong and fit—and here I was.

I fell to pieces, crying right there in the gym bathroom. That number seemed to be quantitative proof that I was a failure.

A tsunami of self-doubt washed over me. *Who am I to be a coach or trainer when I can't even help myself get results?* I thought. *I've gained all this weight back, I'm starting back at zero. Who am I to help other people? Who am I to own an organization called Girls Gone Strong when I can hardly tie my shoes without pain?*

In the coming weeks and months I not only battled these self-critical thoughts but also began receiving a lot of public scrutiny about my body. Strangers, peers, colleagues, and people in the fitness community all seemed to come out of the woodwork to tell me I wasn't good enough.

People commented on my YouTube videos, asking what was wrong with my body and why I didn't look the way that I used to look. Women in my community told other women not to come to my gym because they might end up looking like me. And a male colleague of mine stood in my office and made fun of my body in front of our gym staff.

My solution to fix all of this was to "get my body back," yet again. I hired an online nutrition coach to help me lose body fat, and he sent me weekly meal plans. Each week I sent him my measurements and photos of myself in a bathing suit so he could evaluate my progress and update my meal plan. My meal plan each week was pretty much the same: a small portion of lean meat, steamed veggies, a small sweet potato if I was lucky, and a slice of avocado.

At one point, my progress stalled slightly. I sent my pictures and measurements to my coach, and he responded with an updated meal plan.

Same lean meat. Same steamed veggies. No avocado.

I lost it.

I thought, *Do I really want to spend my life sending pictures of myself in a bathing suit to some guy a couple states over so he can tell me I can't have a fucking slice of avocado?*

The answer—finally, mercifully—was no.

After some deep soul-searching and introspection, I realized that I thought my body had to look a certain way to be valuable and worthy. I felt like my body was the most important thing about me, and no matter what I did, it never measured up.

I was tired of feeling like I wasn't good enough. I was tired of not liking my body. I was tired of feeling like my identity and self-worth were wrapped up in what my body looked like or what it could do. And I was so freakin' tired of feeling like my sense of worthiness could be ripped away from me at any moment.

I was tired of living in *scarcity*. I wanted to feel good about myself and who I was, no matter my size or weight or what I looked like. I wanted to believe my worth was inherent, independent of my body.

I wanted to be free.

So I decided to do something about it.*

Fast-forward eight years, and my life is completely different. I feel good about myself and who I am, and I have a better relationship with my body than ever. It's not that I think my body is perfect—I no longer believe there's even such a thing as a "perfect" body—but I know I am worthy of love, belonging, and respect regardless of how my body looks.

What's more, I have a steadfast sense of self-acceptance, compassion, and inner worth that has nothing to do with my body. I live according to my values,

---

* I'd love to give you the magic solution to healing from body angst, but the truth is it took time, effort, and more detail than I have the space to go into here. If you'd like help getting off the diet and exercise roller coaster or healing your relationship with your body, there's a list of free courses you can take in the Companion Resource Guide that accompanies this book. Visit www.MollyGalbraith.com/book-resources. And of course, keep reading because I'm about to give you some important steps that will help you get started on your journey to kick scarcity mindset.

and I'm proud of the work I do. I feel good in my own skin. I know who I am, and I live according to that truth.

I want the same for you.

Of course, your story won't be the same as mine. Maybe body image is a struggle of yours, and maybe it's not. From the work we do at Girls Gone Strong, we've learned there are other common ways scarcity mindset shows up for women.

Below are ways they say scarcity mindset shows up for them. Check the box if these resonate with you too.

- ☐ I don't want to slow down or take a break because other women might get ahead of me and snag the promotion/job/bonus/approval/etc.
- ☐ I don't feel like I'm doing enough. I feel like I need to do more, give more, help more.
- ☐ I sometimes feel jealous when I see pictures of other women looking happy on social media or when good things happen in their lives.
- ☐ I feel guilty when I do things to take care of myself because I don't want to be seen as "selfish" for taking time away from my family.
- ☐ I feel like other women have it better than me—a nicer house, more travel, well-behaved kids, a better social life.
- ☐ I feel the need to explain myself or justify my actions because if I don't, someone might criticize me, judge me, or blame me.
- ☐ When I'm feeling bad about myself I sometimes opt out of things—important events (e.g., weddings, reunions, baby showers, trips with loved ones), speaking up in meetings, vying for promotions, etc.

Regardless of exactly how these patterns show up for you, I do know this for certain: we can't help others until we help ourselves.

While learning about ourselves and our behaviors is an ongoing journey, there are some things we can do right now to move forward. Through my own experience and the many (many, many) interactions I've had with other women on this subject, I've come to learn there are a couple of crucial steps we must take in order to progress.

First, we need to embrace the "Strong women lift each other up" mindset and commit to creating more opportunities for women. We need to recognize that while we might not be able to miraculously change things overnight, we can make an exponential difference by employing the ripple effect.

Second, we need to push back against scarcity mindset. You already got started with this simply by considering whether the scenarios listed above resonated with you. We can't change what we don't know about, so increasing awareness of your own scarcity mindset is key. To keep going with this, try the worksheet in the "Next Steps" section below.

After that, we've got to start making changes in our lives. That might sound scary, but trust me when I say they're pretty damn awesome. For starters, we've got to get the heck out of that comparison trap that keeps us in constant competition with one another and finally start living true to ourselves and our values.

If you want to learn how to do that, read on.

Next Steps

As I said in chapter 2, how you approach these exercises is up to you. If you want to do each of the exercises at the end of every chapter, that's great! But if you'd rather read the book uninterrupted and circle back later, that works too! (Remember, at the end of the book there's also a checklist to help you keep track of what you've done.)

To do these exercises, you can write directly in the book, or visit www.MollyGalbraith.com/book-resources to download the Companion Resource Guide. In it you'll find printable and fillable PDFs of all the book exercises in one place, among many other resources I've curated for you.

Exercise #1: Recognizing How Scarcity Mindset Shows Up in Your Life

Consider the following questions. Answer yes, no, or maybe to each. If you answer yes or maybe, elaborate as much as you feel comfortable.

Note: If you get stuck or aren't sure, move to the next question. You can always return when the answer comes to you.

1. Do you have any negative thoughts about yourself or your body—e.g., I'm not good enough, other women are ahead of me, I feel guilty when I take care of myself, I hate the way my body looks, I've gained so much weight, etc.?

2. If yes, do these negative thoughts about yourself or your body prevent you from doing things you want to do—e.g., wearing a bathing suit, vying for a promotion, speaking up in a meeting, trying a new fitness class, dating after a breakup?

3. Do you ever stress about your nutrition and exercise—i.e., you feel like you should be dieting or exercising more because you want to look a certain way?

4. Do you ever feel like you "don't measure up" or don't "fit the mold" of what you're supposed to look like or how you're supposed to live your life—e.g., you should look a certain way, you should be further in your career, you should be "settled down," married, or have kids by now, you should be doing or giving more, etc.?

5. Do you ever experience self-doubt or have feelings of impostor syndrome, where you doubt your abilities and worry about being exposed as incapable or a "fraud"—e.g., "they're going to find out I'm not as smart/experienced/talented as they think I am"? If so, when do these feelings arise?

6. What do you do regularly, if anything, to engage in self-care—e.g., get in bed early, move your body, get out in nature, go to therapy, get a massage, etc.? Do you ever feel guilt when you take time to engage in self-care?

If you've answered yes to any of these questions, please know you are not alone. So many women have struggled with scarcity mindset (me included!) and I'm here to tell you: you can overcome it. You'll learn more in the coming chapters. For now, simply notice your experience, and be gentle with yourself.

Exercise #2: Observing Signs of Scarcity Mindset in Others

This exercise is about tuning in to the scarcity mindset around you. The idea is to raise your awareness about how scarcity mindset affects other people and shows up in your environment.

Over the next several days, while you continue to read this book, record when you recognize signs of scarcity mindset.

You might observe examples of it on TV, in movies, on social media, in podcasts or on the radio, at work, in your friend group, at family functions, and even at your place of worship.

You can set a daily reminder on your phone to reflect on your day and note any signs of scarcity mindset you've seen, such as:

- Women speaking negatively about their own bodies
- People commenting on other women's bodies
- People commenting on what women are wearing or what they should/shouldn't wear
- Women talking about the diet they're currently on (or which one they're "cheating" on)
- Women talking about what they are or aren't allowed to eat
- Women expressing guilt about or justifying things they do to care for themselves
- People gossiping about or talking down about other women

Once again, try not to judge. Scarcity mindset affects all of us, and judging or criticizing others for it doesn't help. Instead, by noticing, naming, and recording what you see and hear, you'll gain a greater awareness of all the ways scarcity mindset seeps into your life. And this awareness will lay a foundation for you to begin overcoming scarcity mindset.

If you prefer to keep your notes here, we've provided the space below for you.

Signs of scarcity mindset I've seen:

CHAPTER 4

Overcoming Comparison and Jealousy

Life is not a zero-sum game. There's room for everyone. I love seeing other people doing their thing, operating in their zone of genius, and learning from them. It's a great time to be alive. The possibilities are endless.

—DR. SHANTÉ COFIELD

CHAPTER 4

Overcoming Comparison and Jealousy

You know the type. Thick, flowing hair. Naturally tanned skin. Lean, lightly muscled body. And the face of a beauty queen.

It wasn't just her looks either. She had it all. A handsome husband. Beautiful home. Strength, smarts, and *lots* of attention.

We both worked in the fitness industry, and it seemed like she always got the recognition, opportunities, and praise that I wanted. We were friends. Sort of. Whenever her name came up in conversation, I always smiled and nodded along.

"Jen? Oh yeah, she's great."

But the truth is, I was jealous of her—painfully jealous. All I could see was what she had and what I didn't have. I was embarrassed and ashamed for feeling that way. I *liked* her. Why did I care so much about what she had? Why couldn't I be happy with what I had?

Unfortunately, my jealousy got worse before it got better.

One day, I learned that Jen had been selected to join a training team for a well-known fitness education company. Careerwise, this was huge. As a team member, Jen would get tons of attention and build her industry cred. Plus, she'd receive sponsorship from the company, which meant she'd get cool clothing, supplements, equipment, and more.

There had been more than one opening on the team, but by the time I learned all this, applications were already closed.

I freaked.

I had desperately wanted that opportunity for years but didn't know applications were open—much less already closed. Heart racing and palms sweating,

I scrambled to reach out to the head of the company and beg for an interview. He granted me one, and I was over the moon.

This was my chance.

The day of the interview came. It was a phone interview. Thank goodness for that because I was sweating through my clothes.

At the end of the interview, the woman on the phone thanked me for my time. Then she said something I didn't want to hear. "I'm sorry, Molly. You're great, but you won't be getting an invite because you're too similar to another team member we just brought on."

Dagger.

I went to work that night at the restaurant where I was waiting tables to make ends meet. Every time I was out of the customers' line of sight, I'd cry. It felt like my world had come crashing down and I'd missed the biggest opportunity of my life.

What's more, my fears had been confirmed. I wasn't good enough, and Jen was better than me.

It's not that I didn't want Jen to do well, but every time she had success, it shined a spotlight on my perceived failures and insecurities.

To be honest, Jen wasn't an exception. I compared myself to lots of other women too—friends, family members, acquaintances, colleagues, women on social media or in magazines. I was sizing myself up against all of them.

I didn't realize it at the time, but I was caught in The Comparison Trap.

Welcome to The Comparison Trap

The Comparison Trap is a huge part of the scarcity story we tell ourselves—we're not enough, and there's not enough to go around.

The Comparison Trap is emotional quicksand. It makes you feel like no matter what you have, it's never enough. According to your perception, there's always someone fitter, prettier, happier, or more successful.

We're caught in The Comparison Trap when we compare ourselves to other women. We compare our bodies, our kids, our jobs, our relationships, our travel, our net worth, our clothing, our whole lives to other women, particularly those we see on social media.

Sometimes comparison isn't even about other women—it's about our own lives and bodies and where we think we "should" be.

That was certainly the case for me. For the first nine years of my fitness journey, I took hundreds of pictures of myself in the same bathing suit, position, and lighting, week after week. I meticulously searched for ways my body had changed, hoping to see that my hard work had paid off and that I'd lost fat or gained muscle. How I looked in those pictures would determine how I felt about myself for the rest of the day (or week).

Even worse, those pictures led me to live in a state of limbo, constantly thinking about where I was trying to get to rather than appreciating the present moment.

There's nothing wrong with taking pictures to see how nutrition or exercise affects your body, if that's your thing. For me, what was problematic was viewing those pictures as a "before." I had this persistent idea that the "after" would be some kind of perfect situation where I finally had the life and body of my dreams. Until I arrived there, I couldn't be truly happy.

Whether you're busy comparing yourself to others, or to some "before" or "after" state, you're in the throes of The Comparison Trap.

Are You Caught in The Comparison Trap?

Sometimes these patterns are so ingrained they can be hard to recognize in ourselves. But recognizing them is the first step toward change.

If you're unsure whether you're caught in The Comparison Trap, here's a quick quiz you can take to find out.

If you answer yes to any of the following questions, check the corresponding box.

Do you compare yourself to other women in any of these categories?

- ☐ bodies
- ☐ families
- ☐ kids
- ☐ jobs
- ☐ travel
- ☐ clothing
- ☐ relationships
- ☐ finances
- ☐ other

- ☐ Do you compare yourself to a past version of yourself ("I was way fitter/leaner/happier back then" or "I wish I could get back to my old jean size/college weight")?
- ☐ Do you compare yourself to a future version of yourself ("When I lose these ten pounds or get this promotion, then I'll be happy")?
- ☐ Do you ever scroll through social media and feel jealous or insecure?
- ☐ Do you ever feel jealous or insecure during a catch-up with one of your friends?
- ☐ When your peers or colleagues have success or accomplish something big, do you ever struggle to feel truly happy for them?

If you answered yes to any of these questions, you need to know two things:

IT'S OKAY. You don't have to feel ashamed or bad about yourself for having those thoughts or feelings. They're normal—but they also kind of suck, for everyone involved. Which leads me to point number two . . .

YOU DON'T HAVE TO FEEL THIS WAY. These feelings are all part of The Comparison Trap. They're also part of the scarcity mindset that plagues so many women. But to become the strong, awesome, fully realized badass I know you can be, you must get out of The Comparison Trap.

And yes, you can get out of it (don't worry—I'll show you how). First, let's try to better understand The Comparison Trap.

What Does The Comparison Trap Feel Like?

The Comparison Trap can be sneaky, popping up in our lives in different ways. Some women in our community shared how The Comparison Trap affects their lives. Can you relate to any of these experiences?

Feeling Bad about Your Body, Weight, or Eating Habits

"It is easy to fall into the comparison trap on any social media platform. At one point, I was so deep in my own body dysmorphia that I couldn't stop scrolling through all these 'flawless' women's Instagram profiles. I would look at them and then nitpick my body apart and wonder what wasn't good enough about my body that it couldn't look like theirs. I ended up unfollowing over twenty-five women who I admired in the fitness community because of my inability to see my self-worth in my own skin." —Sierra

"For me, the comparison always comes around food. Like, 'So-and-so can eat whatever she wants and not worry' or 'How can she eat so much junk food and yet never put on weight?' I hate that I feel that way. And I know that everyone has a journey; goodness knows how these women feel about themselves or what their eating/non-eating is like behind closed doors. Still, it's hard not to compare, especially when I'm feeling down on my own goals." —Laura

Comparing Yourself to Other People in Your Industry or Community

"Teaching dance in a competitive environment, I'm constantly comparing myself to other teachers and comparing my students to their students. I am trying hard to teach my students that another team can be amazing without extinguishing our flame, but it's a long process, especially when I struggle with jealousy/comparing myself." —Amanda

Feeling Like You're Not Where You "Should Be"

"I often fall into the comparison trap, usually when I am feeling shame for not being where I 'should be.' I often feel like I have to justify my current workouts/fitness and explain that I'm struggling with injuries and muscular issues. It's hard. On top of that, I tend to feel that other women don't like me or are judging me." —Jeannette

Wanting to Be Faster, Stronger, or Fitter

"I grew up playing sports and have struggled with competitiveness. If a friend gets started before me at the gym or is lifting more than me, I find myself getting down instead of being inspired by their success." —Layla

Thinking Other People Are More Successful and Have More

"When I see other women more successful than I am, with better jobs and better cars, sometimes it's hard not to be jealous and wish that I had what they had." —Angelika

Why Are We So Prone to Comparison?

Comparing ourselves to others is a natural impulse that's part of the brain's social-cognition network. Humans are social creatures who are adept at sizing one another up, seeing where we fit, and establishing hierarchy. And it's not always a bad thing.

In fact, comparing can sometimes be useful, like when someone else's achievements help you feel motivated or inspired. For example: if you see your friend run a marathon and think, *You know, that's something I want to do!* You may feel a tinge of envy, sure, but you don't feel ill will toward her. Instead, you ask her for advice on how to work toward your new goal.

Other examples include the following: If you're in salary negotiations, knowing if you're making above or below the median salary for someone in your position can give you leverage. If you're applying for a competitive job, knowing what qualifications the other applicants have can give you insight into where you may need to level up your skills or experience. Or if you have a specific performance goal you want to achieve—e.g., place in your age group in an athletic competition—knowing what numbers you need to hit is critical to achieve your goal.

But this isn't the kind of comparison I'm talking about. I'm talking about the kind of comparison that goes hand in hand with scarcity mindset.

The dark side of comparison is when it leads to feelings of jealousy and shame.

Unlike admiration, which can foster a desire to emulate another person's success, jealousy—or more accurately, envy—can breed resentment and a desire to compete with or outdo other women.

When we see the best parts of other people's lives and compare them to our everyday lives, the story we end up telling ourselves is that we aren't good enough, we don't measure up, everyone else is doing it better than we are, and there must be something wrong with us.

That story might go something like this:

Envy and Shame Spiral

Shame spirals, like the one above, can happen within seconds—especially when this thought process is a habit. Our brain automatically repeats the same process it's used to, which for many women happens multiple times per day.

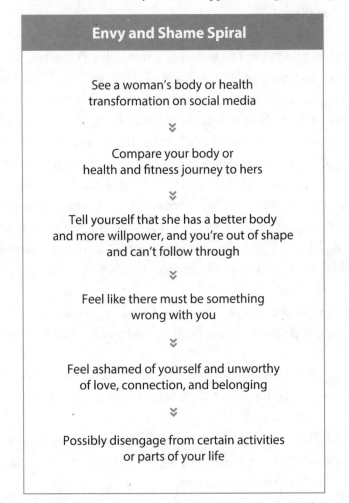

Envy and Shame Spiral

See a woman's body or health transformation on social media

⌄

Compare your body or health and fitness journey to hers

⌄

Tell yourself that she has a better body and more willpower, and you're out of shape and can't follow through

⌄

Feel like there must be something wrong with you

⌄

Feel ashamed of yourself and unworthy of love, connection, and belonging

⌄

Possibly disengage from certain activities or parts of your life

The Comparison Trap is particularly challenging in the era of social media.[1] Today's media culture has a comparison-inducing effect on us for a few reasons.

For one thing, we're consuming more media than ever before. According to

Nielsen, American adults spend more than eleven hours a day interacting with media, and much of that is social media.[2]

What's more, we have access to whatever we want, whenever we want. Feeling insecure in your relationship? You can go down a three-hour rabbit hole looking at everything your partner's ex ever posted. Feeling like your body doesn't measure up? With the touch of a button, you can access endless photos and videos of women with seemingly perfect bodies, which you can tell yourself you're looking at for "inspiration" but may leave you feeling worse about yourself. The same with any topic. You can spend hours reading, watching, and consuming content that leads you to feeling worse about yourself.

And the problem of comparison is about more than just the sheer volume of media we're consuming.

The Comparison Trap and High Expectations

For all that we've yet to achieve, there's no doubt that women have gained more equality and opportunity over the past decades. At the same time, many women in the GGS community have expressed that they feel like the expectation for what they "should" be able to do and achieve has increased too. They've said they feel like they're expected to have a high-powered career, marry and have children, be a great friend/mother/boss/employee, "get their body back" within six weeks of having a baby, handle the majority of the unpaid domestic labor at home—plus find time to exercise, drink enough water, prepare home-cooked meals, have a great sex life, remember everyone's birthday, and volunteer in the community.

I read recently that in America we ask mothers "to work like they don't have children and mother like they don't work outside the home."[3]

Oof.

Social media, celebrity culture, marketing, television shows, and other forms of media can emphasize this message, intentionally or not. Many of these outlets present unrealistic bodies, lives, relationships, careers, and children.

This isn't to say you shouldn't set high standards for yourself if that's what you want. Go after what's most important to you. But recognize that if you have a nagging sense of never being good enough, you may be placing unreasonable expectations on yourself.

The Comparison Trap and Scarcity

The lack of opportunities and scarcity mindset that women face can easily translate into feelings of jealousy or frustration against women who *do* achieve those coveted chances—like the colleague who scores the promotion in your male-dominated field or the one female speaker invited to be on the panel at a popular conference.

Comedian and actress Ali Wong explained the situation perfectly with this anecdote:

> When the movie *Crazy Rich Asians* premiered, a very talented Asian American actress in her late forties admitted to me that she refused to watch the film and would probably never see it, simply because she was jealous that she wasn't in it. As she looked down at her shoes, she confessed, "I just feel so left out." The lack of opportunities for Asian Americans in Hollywood had conditioned her to feel insecure and envious.[4]

Those experiences or opportunities you desire may indeed feel scarce. But the idea that we *must* compete within this limited range of opportunities is *false*.

Ultimately, The Comparison Trap not only hurts us but also prevents us from lifting one another up.

Think about it. If you view another woman as your competition—as someone who can take your place or prevent you from getting what you want:

- Might you be less likely to share and support her work?
- Might you be less likely to feel happy for her and celebrate her?
- Might you be less likely to recommend or endorse her?
- Might you struggle developing a deep, meaningful relationship with her?

I'm willing to bet the answer is yes.

On the other hand, if you adopt the "Strong women lift each other up" philosophy, you can choose to stop competing with other women and lift them up instead.

That's what my friend Jennifer Lau did.

As Jennifer explains, "In 2018 it was brought to my attention that a big sportswear brand was hosting an event to highlight the top female fitness professionals in Toronto. And there wasn't a single Woman of Color invited."

This event was the tipping point after many panels, events, and campaigns that "didn't feature any Women of Color. . . . It was like, enough's enough."

A successful and seasoned fitness professional herself, Jennifer could have tried to duke it out and fight with other women for a spot among the existing events. Instead, she teamed up with her friend and fellow fitness pro Jela Tubei. "We thought, *Why don't we do our own event and see what happens?*"

As they put the event together, Jennifer and Jela deliberately supported Women of Color at every opportunity. "We wanted a venue that was owned and operated by someone of color, and a DJ that was a Woman of Color. A photographer. A caterer. It was all Women of Color."

Their event, The Real Toronto, brought together professionals in fitness, health, and wellness for a workout and networking opportunity. The initial event sold out in less than a week, and funds raised went to Sistering Toronto, a local women's shelter. Since its inception, it's grown into a quarterly event, with bigger impact than they ever imagined.

"Big brands have been scrolling through our social media and reaching out to the attendees of our events, and Jela has been compiling a list of women who want more opportunities, and those brands have been reaching out to get access to the list because they're looking for more diverse professionals to work with."

Jela added, "It opened up opportunities for Women of Color who were struggling to find jobs in studios and gyms to network, and many of them have now successfully begun their careers as personal trainers and yoga instructors."

And it's not just the attendees. More opportunities are rolling in for the photographer and the DJ, and more sales are coming in for the vendors.

This is *exactly* the kind of ripple effect you can create when you choose to step out of comparison and lift women up instead.

The Comparison Trap Is Escapable

Jennifer is proof that The Comparison Trap is escapable, and so am I. My life is better and happier now, not because I've achieved some "after" body and not because I've become "better" than the women I compare myself to.

Quite the opposite. Life is better now because I've embraced who I am and because I embrace other women's successes.

I still do compare (we all do—it's a natural human process), but I feel good about that comparison because I'm able to view it objectively and use it to improve. Comparison affirms my own values and direction while allowing me to genuinely enjoy and appreciate the success and happiness of other women. Their accomplishments motivate and inspire me, and it feels like they're lighting the path for me to get that same thing if I want to.

Remember Jen, from the beginning of the chapter? The one I was so jealous of? Today, she's one of my best friends and colleagues. In fact, she's a Girls Gone Strong cofounder and the head coach of our GGS Coaching program for women.

When I told Jen about this book, she freaked out (in the best way) and said, "I have the happiest pang of jealousy ever right now because this has always been one of my goals for myself. I'm so proud of you! You deserve this, and I can't wait to read it."

This embodies everything I've talked about in this chapter. Jen was able to feel her feelings: happiness, joy, excitement, *and* a pang of jealousy. She identified where that jealousy came from (she wants to write a book too) and allowed her envy to spark her own motivation while feeling happy for me.

To take this idea a step further, if Jen decides to write her own book, she has a friend and confidante to share experiences, make critical introductions, and support her through the process.

This is a great example of how lifting other women up and celebrating their successes can result in our own future success.

Four Techniques to Get Out of The Comparison Trap

I used four powerful techniques to overcome my struggles with comparison and jealousy. You can use these to get out of The Comparison Trap too.

In my experience, these techniques take some practice. But the more you use them, the better they work.

Technique #1: Notice and Name

A few years ago, I went to a post-church brunch with my Gama and some of her friends. As soon as our server left, the women at the table, all between the ages of sixty and eighty, started talking.

"Oh gosh! You just eat like a bird, don't you?"

"You're so lucky you can eat like that and maintain your figure."

"I'm going to be a pig today and get a soup *and* salad."

The women talked like this for the next ten minutes.

Holy crap! I thought to myself. *It never stops. It never, ever stops.*

This group of smart, progressive, gracious, kind, accomplished women were still worried about:

- what they were eating—and what they weren't eating
- what their friends were eating—and what their friends weren't eating
- the size and shape of their bodies—and the size and shape of their friends' bodies

Somehow, I thought the whole obsession with food and bodies and comparing ourselves to others and feeling fundamentally not enough magically stopped when women got older.

But it doesn't. The Comparison Trap is so pervasive that it's automatic, and we don't even realize we're doing it. It's insidious and will plague us until the day we die if we let it. The only way for it to stop is for us to make it stop.

Stopping this ingrained pattern begins by noticing and naming.

"Notice and name" is a concept we use in our GGS Coaching program. Borrowed from the field of psychology, the "notice and name" approach raises awareness, and evidence also suggests it helps reduce the intensity of our emotions.[5]

Notice and name works exactly like it sounds: you notice when certain thoughts, words, or behaviors happen and label them for what they are.

You may recognize some of the following scarcity mindset patterns in yourself:

COMMON SCARCITY MINDSET PATTERNS		
Thoughts & Feelings	**Words**	**Actions**
You think about all the ways other women are better than you. When you scroll through social media, you feel jealous of colleagues or friends.	You gossip behind people's backs or inadvertently spread rumors by saying things like, "I don't know if it's true, but I heard . . ."	You avoid doing things like speaking up in groups, saying yes to projects, or leading at working because you don't feel qualified.
You feel like you don't "fit the mold" or that you need to look a certain way or wear a certain size to be accepted or "fit in" with your friends or colleagues.	You speak negatively about yourself when good things happen to others. Someone's happy Facebook post sends you into a spiral of wondering, *What's wrong with me?*	You don't feel "good enough" to pursue things you want. You're not "experi-enced enough" to go for that new job or not "fit enough" to go to the gym or try a new workout class.
You have a hard time feeling genuinely happy for others—perhaps because it triggers your own insecurity, jealousy, or anxiety.	You dismiss women's "successes" and share your opinion on how they got what they have (new car, job promotion, health transformation).	You're hesitant to help other women for fear they might get ahead of you or get opportunities you want.
You focus on what you think other women do "wrong"—how they're parenting, working, caring for others, planning their wedding, exercising, or eating, etc.	You judge other women out loud, sharing all the ways you think they're falling short, messing up, or not doing it "right."	You spend your time and energy trying to fix, correct, or police others and their behavior, or you give unsolicited opinions.

As you recognize these patterns, try not to judge or criticize. Beating yourself up makes things worse, not better! When practicing the "notice and name" technique, aim to become more aware. Awareness is the first crucial step toward change.

Technique #2: Think of Comparison as a Mirror, Not a Window

Occasionally, I still compare myself to other women in a negative way, often when I'm going through an emotionally difficult or stressful time. Luckily, after more than a decade of therapy, I've learned that this tendency has nothing to do with the other person and everything to do with me.

My dear friend, author, and Whole30 CEO Melissa Urban (whose ability to be introspective never fails to amaze me) says that "judgment is a mirror, not a window."[6] I think this analogy can be applied to comparison as well.

Comparison is a mirror, not a window.

Meaning, when we compare ourselves to other people, it's not actually about them. It's typically a reflection of where we're struggling with our own insecurities or desires. Framed this way, it can be easier to let go of jealous or resentful feelings and instead focus on moving toward the kind of life you want for yourself. (More on how to do this later in the book.)

Technique #3: Learn to Separate Their "Highlight Reel" from Your "Behind the Scenes"

For many of us, The Comparison Trap shows up when we compare our "behind the scenes" to someone else's "highlight reel."

This is especially true with social media. As you scroll through someone's feed, you see picture-perfect scenes, a carefully curated view of someone's life. You see the weddings, birthdays, new houses, trips, and holiday celebrations. What you don't see are all the trade-offs and associated costs.

Maybe your friend is married to a gorgeous doctor, but she's lonely in their beautiful home all by herself. Maybe your former college roommate has a fancy job and makes a ton of money, but she works eighty hours a week and desperately wants time to relax. Maybe your work colleague has abs of steel, but she engages in disordered eating habits and wishes she could let loose and enjoy herself with food once in a while.

This doesn't mean that everyone who seems happy is secretly miserable. And it *definitely* doesn't mean that women don't deserve to be loving, and celebrating, every bit of their lives. The point is that we can't know everything about another woman's life from looking at her social media or chatting with her at a monthly book club meeting.

Another problem with making comparisons based on someone's highlight reel is that we tend to leave our values out of the equation.

Let's say you value spending time with your friends. You might look at your successful college roommate and think, *Gee, that looks like an amazing job! I'm so jealous of her achievements.* But what you don't know is that she sacrifices a lot of social time for her job—a trade-off you wouldn't be willing to make.

Consider the other side of things: Imagine your former college roommate scrolls through Instagram and feels a tinge of jealousy at all the pictures of friends hanging out. She's decided to focus on her career, and she knows that means she'll sometimes miss out on social events. Still, she can't help but think, *I wish I could be there. They look like they're having so much fun.*

Comparison, jealousy, and shame can happen instantaneously. But if we saw someone else's behind-the-scenes life, we would maybe find we don't want what they have.

However, if we *do* want what they have—like I mentioned above—these feelings can be used to help guide you toward your dreams (more on how to do that later).

Technique #4: Run Comparison and Jealousy through Your "Values Filter"

In the next chapter, you'll learn about values: what they are, how to find yours, and how they can guide your decision-making to ensure you're living true to yourself and in a way that makes you proud.

For now, here's a glimpse into the idea of a "values filter" and how it can help you get out of The Comparison Trap.

You can use the values filter to find out whether you truly want what that other person has. If you do, you can shift away from jealousy and start working toward what you want. And if you don't, this realization can soften the jealousy, provide some perspective, and allow you to move on.

VALUES FILTER

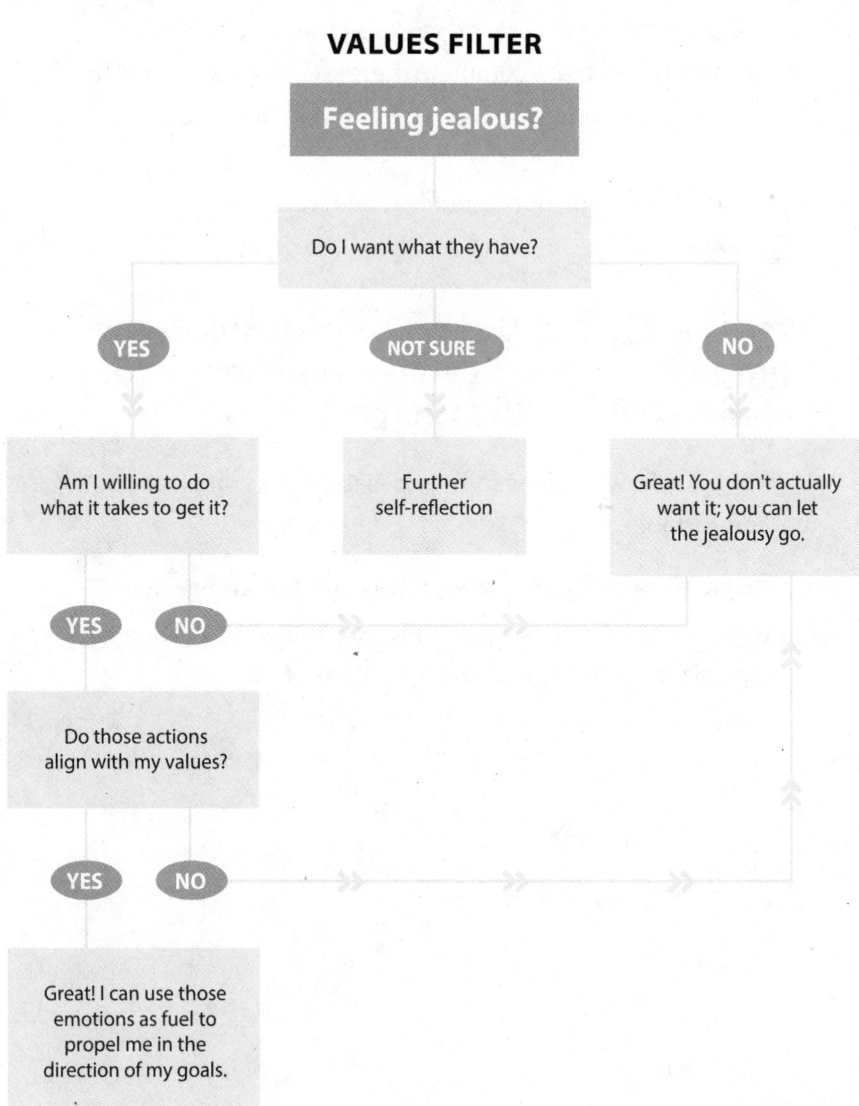
Feeling jealous?
Do I want what they have?
YES
NOT SURE
NO
Am I willing to do what it takes to get it?
Further self-reflection
Great! You don't actually want it; you can let the jealousy go.
YES
NO
Do those actions align with my values?
YES
NO
Great! I can use those emotions as fuel to propel me in the direction of my goals.

Next Steps

Earlier in the chapter you took a little quiz about the comparison trap and read several examples of how scarcity mindset can show up in your life. Now we're going to dig a little deeper. You can get started immediately, complete these exercises once you've finished the book, or return whenever it's right for you.

To download your resource guide, visit:
www.MollyGalbraith.com/book-resources

Exercise #1: Recognizing Jealousy, Comparison, and Scarcity Mindset in Your Relationships with Others

Answer the following questions, and elaborate as much as you feel comfortable.

1. Do you ever compare yourself to or feel jealous of other women? Who are you comparing yourself with? What are you typically comparing and feeling jealous of?

2. Do you worry or feel anxious that female friends or colleagues might get ahead of you or get opportunities you want? If so, what are you thinking and feeling when that happens?

3. Do you ever struggle to feel truly happy when something good happens to a friend or colleague—e.g., when they get a promotion, start dating a great person, go on an awesome vacation, or have success in their career? If so, what are you thinking and feeling when that happens?

4. Do you ever find yourself gossiping about, making fun of, putting down, or judging someone behind her back? If so, when does this happen, and how are you feeling when you do it?

Exercise #2: Observe How and When Jealousy, Comparison, and Scarcity Mindset Show Up in Your Life

This exercise is about tuning in to your own comparison, jealousy, and scarcity mindset in the moment and using your feelings as a mirror to be introspective and learn more about yourself.

- What am I doing or who am I with when these feelings of comparison and jealousy arise—e.g., watching TV, scrolling through social media, talking to a coworker, attending a family dinner, etc.?
- What am I comparing or feeling jealous of—e.g., someone else's body, hair, relationship, job, success, children, finances, happiness, etc.?
- How does this make me feel—e.g., like I'm not good enough, jealous of them, annoyed at them, like I'm falling behind, etc.?
- What do I do when this happens—e.g., stop engaging with what's making me feel bad, torture myself by consuming more of what makes me jealous, berate myself for what I'm not or what I don't have, gossip or talk down about the woman I'm feeling jealous of, numb my feelings with food or alcohol, etc.?

You can set a daily reminder on your phone to reflect on your day and make notes of any signs of comparison and jealousy you've experienced.

When you notice these feelings, try not to judge yourself. Comparison and jealousy affect almost everyone from time to time, and judging yourself isn't useful. Instead, by noticing, naming, and recording what you're experiencing, you'll gain a greater awareness of how comparison and jealousy show up in your life—the first step to overcoming this tendency.

If you prefer to keep your notes here, we've provided space below for you.

Notes about comparison, and jealousy, and scarcity mindset I've experienced this week:

CHAPTER 5

Living True to Yourself

We are not what other people say we are. We are who we know ourselves to be, and we are what we love.

—LAVERNE COX

CHAPTER 5

Living True to Yourself

"Woman in U.S. Likes Her Body"

That was the headline the year I made international news.[1]

In December 2015, I was walking with my partner, Casey, on the beach in Costa Rica, and he took a picture of me in my bathing suit.

A couple weeks later, on New Year's Day, a realization hit me like a ton of bricks.

This is the first year in as long as I can remember that I haven't made a New Year's resolution to change the way my body looks.

I pulled out my phone and started writing a social media post using that photo of me on the beach.

This is what I wrote:

> This is my body.
>
> This is not a before picture. This is not an after picture.
>
> This just happens to be what my body looks like on a random Tuesday in December of 2015—it's a *life* picture.
>
> This is a body that loves protein and vegetables and queso and ice cream. This is a body that loves bent presses* and pull-ups and deadlifts and sleep.
>
> This is a body that has been abused with fast food and late nights and stress. This is a body that has been pushed to the brink of leanness in figure competitions and maximum strength in powerlifting meets. This is a body that begged for mercy when it was diagnosed with Hashimoto's and PCOS.
>
> This is a body that has been called:

* Yes, I mean *bent press*, not *bench press*. It's an awesome exercise. Google it.

- too fat
- too thin
- too masculine
- too strong
- too weak
- too big
- too skinny

. . . all within the same week.

This body has been publicly evaluated, judged, and criticized, and those judgments have been used to determine my level of skill as a coach and a trainer, and my worth as a person, both positively and negatively.

Some people say they would "kill to have this body." Others say they would "kill themselves if they had this body." (Yes, unfortunately, that's actually a thing humans say to one another.)

This is a body that I spent too much time, energy, and mental space wishing would look different.

And today?

Today this is a body that is loved, adored, and cherished by the only person whose opinion matters—*me.*

This is the first year in as long as I can remember that I have made *no* resolutions to change the way my body looks.

This is a kind of freedom I didn't think I'd ever experience, and it feels really, really good.[2]

Almost immediately after I hit publish, I refreshed the page. My post had 57 likes.

Huh? I hit refresh again and saw it had climbed to 236 likes.

Wait, what? After another refresh it was at 552 likes.

Within minutes, the post had thousands of likes. Over the next couple of weeks, across all outlets, it reached a whopping 464 million people worldwide. It was featured on the *Today* show website and in *People* magazine and shared by A-list celebrities as diverse as Ashton Kutcher, Lil Wayne, Zooey Deschanel, and George Takei.

I was thrilled that my message resonated with so many folks, but it's not like I'd done some kind of record-breaking physical feat or come up with some sort of life-changing invention.

Nope. *I basically made international news because I said I liked my body and didn't want to change it.*

I never expected that single post to get so much attention. But I was surprised by what followed: a slew of intensely negative feedback, particularly from women.

"Who does she think she is?"

"She needs to lose forty pounds. Then she can talk."

"Don't be so full of yourself."

I also was called names like *whore*, *attention whore*, and *slut*.

The public's reaction to my declaration of self-acceptance made something clear to me. As much as we pay lip service to the idea of self-love, positivity, or success, many women are criticized and shamed the moment they seem to like, love, or celebrate themselves "too much."

"Love Your Body, but Not Too Much"

As women, it can feel like we're constantly receiving messages about what we're supposed to be—the "right" way to be a woman, if you will.

These messages are communicated through movies, TV, music lyrics and videos, social media, family members, friends, teachers, worship leaders, and more. And they're often contradictory and can make it feel impossible to "get it right." These messages show up in numerous ways. Here are several instances I've personally witnessed:

- Be thin, but not too skinny.
- Be toned, but not too muscular.
- Be curvy and womanly, but not fat.
- Be confident, but not conceited.
- Love your body, but don't be full of yourself.

The media is filled with lean women, and our society is obsessed with fat loss, yet a woman who is too thin by someone else's subjective standards will be told she "needs to eat a cheeseburger" or someone will whisper behind her back, "Ugh . . . gross."

We tell women to be confident, but when a woman walks into a room with her head held high, sure of who she is and not seeking validation from anyone else, we often scoff and ask, "Who does she think she is? What makes her so special?" We preach messages of "loving yourself" and "loving your body," yet when a woman shows up comfortable in her body, we think she's too full of herself or start picking apart her body or tearing her down to make sure she doesn't love herself "too much."

And it's not just our bodies. Women we work with at GGS have told us they receive other conflicting messages too. You should:

- Be smart, but not a know-it-all.
- Be assertive, but not aggressive.
- Be strong, but not abrasive.
- Be professional, but not cold.
- Be beautiful, but don't try too hard.
- Speak up, but don't talk too much.
- Make sure you smile, but don't be giggly.
- Be kind, but not a pushover.
- Be a leader, but not too bossy.
- Be personable, but don't show too much emotion.
- Be sexy, but not slutty. And *definitely* don't be a tease.

It's. Freaking. Exhausting. And impossible.

And these are the messages I've received as a tall, fit, young, white, blonde-haired, well-educated, heterosexual, cisgender woman. This list doesn't even begin to include the criticisms, standards, judgments, prejudices, and other unfairness heaped upon Black women, Indigenous women, Women of Color, older women, queer women, trans women, fat women, and women with disabilities or fewer socioeconomic resources.* No wonder many of us don't have the time, energy, or capacity to figure out what we really want for ourselves.

* I typically try to use person-first language like "woman with disabilities" instead of "disabled woman" to clarify what a woman "has" versus what she "is." Person-first language can help reduce stigma, marginalization, and dehumanization. Further, I no longer believe that "fat" is a bad word, and I'm following the lead of many fat activists in intentionally using that term to help destigmatize it.

Starting now, I want to make a deal with you. I'm going to give you the tools—and I want you to give yourself the permission—to live life according to *your* wants and *your* values. Deal?

Letting go of what you've been taught and forging your own path might seem scary. But it's worth it.

In Bronnie Ware's book *The Top Five Regrets of the Dying: A Life Transformed by the Dearly Departing*, she found that the number-one regret among people on their deathbeds was this: "I wish I'd had the courage to live a life true to myself, not the life others expected of me." Ware wrote, "This was the most common regret of all. When people realise that their life is almost over and look back clearly on it, it is easy to see how many dreams have gone unfulfilled. Most people had not honoured even a half of their dreams and had to die knowing that it was due to choices they had made, or not made."[3]

Do not let this be you.

Yes, defying others' expectations and living true to yourself can be hard. You are capable of doing hard things. I believe in you.**

"Lift Women Up—But Do It My Way"

When you're doing the important work of lifting women up, other folks will try to place their expectations on you.

Here's what you have to remember:

- There's no playbook for this, and no "right" way to lift women up. We will all do it differently, and that's okay because we need many unique gifts, talents, and skills to create massive change.
- Life is coming at you through the windshield, and you have to make decisions in the moment about what to do. Other people will see your decisions in the rearview mirror with

** As a recovering people pleaser, I understand how powerful "having permission" is as a catalyst for creating change. It's my hope that as you move through this book, you'll continue to realize the only permission you need is your own.

more context and clarity and possibly criticize the decisions you made. (As I've personally experienced, this is especially true if you're in a position of leadership or in the public eye.) You cannot avoid this. Do the best you can, learn from your mistakes, and stay committed to doing better next time.

» All feedback is useful because it gives you the chance to get curious and view another perspective and often pushes you to do better. That said, as long as you know you're living and making decisions true to your values, you'll feel proud of and at peace with your decisions.

The Magic of Living True to You

There is nothing like living true to yourself.

Knowing that your thoughts, your actions, your decisions, and your environment are aligned with what you value most? That, my friend, is priceless.

This reality can seem unattainable, but I have three powerful strategies for you that will help:

- Discover your true values.
- Retrain your brain.
- Curate your environment.

I'm not exaggerating when I say these strategies revolutionized my life. They helped me feel proud of myself and how I live. They helped me feel steadfast in my decisions when others questioned them. And they helped me push back against all the conflicting social pressures that say we, as women, are not enough and we aren't "doing it right."

They can help you do the same.

You can use these strategies throughout your life. Once you get comfortable using them, you can come back to them every time you need to make a tough decision or need a reset.

Strategy #1: Discover Your True Values

Your values are the ingredients you think are important for a good life—the principles you want to live by and the things that matter most to you.

When you live in alignment with and make decisions according to your values, your chances of living a happy, fulfilled, and meaningful life significantly increase. Yet many never take the time or receive the guidance to reflect on and decide what's important to them. And that's unfortunate because you must know what's important to you before you can live in alignment with those values.

As cofounder of a global mission-based movement, every day I have to make tough decisions that come with big trade-offs, and there is no shortage of people who want to share their opinions on those decisions.

We've always wanted GGS to feel like a "we" movement that our members can take ownership and pride in being a part of. They commit to living out the mission, become ambassadors for the movement, and invite others to join.

But this level of participation can also be challenging at times because everyone has an opinion of how Girls Gone Strong should be run and what we

Opinion	Opposing Opinion
GGS has to tackle important topics like discrimination, harassment, abuse, and racism because they deeply affect women's health and cannot be separated from the other topics you talk about in our community (e.g., mental health, sexual health, pre-and postnatal health, access to healthful food and safe places to move your body). If you don't cover these topics, GGS is just another organization that doesn't really care about all women.	I didn't come here for politics. I came to GGS for fitness. I can see politics anywhere else I look these days. I just want to learn more about how to get stronger and now I have to wade through all this other junk. I'm disappointed GGS has decided to go in a political direction.

Opinion	Opposing Opinion
If you refuse to talk about fat loss, you're shaming women who have fat loss goals for themselves, and you're not giving women the space to be autonomous beings who make decisions for themselves.	If you discuss fat loss, you're alienating women in larger bodies and buying into the anti-fat bias, fat shaming, diet culture mentality that leads to disordered eating and eating disorders, and you're harming women.
I can't believe how much GGS charges for the programs. I thought accessibility to information was important to you. If you really cared about helping women, you'd make your programs cheaper.	I sure hope you pay your female employees appropriately for their work and offer great benefits, health insurance, paid parental leave, and plenty of vacation time at GGS.

should do. Here are some examples of community members' thoughts. As you'll see, for every opinion (left column), there's an opposing opinion (right column).

For years I lived my life and ran my businesses without getting clear on my values and therefore experienced a lot of turmoil, confusion, and indecisiveness. It was incredibly stressful to make decisions. I second-guessed myself constantly and often felt burned out, torn between competing commitments, and plagued by worry that I wasn't making the right choices.

Identifying my values has allowed me to have more clarity in my decision-making. It also has allowed us leaders at GGS to be transparent with our community about how and why we make some of our decisions so they feel more connected to GGS and our mission.

This doesn't mean we're doing it perfectly. Lifting women up isn't always easy. But having clarity around our top value at GGS of "having the biggest impact while doing the least harm," gives me the peace to know we're living true to ourselves.

Defining Your Values

Taking time to identify your values is a big step, but the process is worth the effort.

In particular, determining your top three values—thinking about them critically and listing them—will not only help you in your work, it will help you get more comfortable with who you are and help you stop comparing yourself to and feeling jealous of other women.

Finding your values is all about understanding what makes you feel:

- happiest
- proud of and good about yourself
- fulfilled and satisfied
- energized, content, or full of vitality and "flow"

When you have clarity on these things, you can deliberately act in accordance with your values, which can in turn inform every area of your life: work, relationships with others, your relationship with yourself and your body, decisions, priorities, and more.

I did my first formal values assessment with my friend and social justice educator Dr. Tee Williams, who educated me and several members of the GGS team about personal and professional values and led us through a values-finding exercise. I've also learned a lot about values from my good friend and mentor Dr. John Berardi (also known as "JB"), cofounder of Precision Nutrition and founder of Change Maker Academy. The values-defining exercise you'll find at the end of this chapter is an amalgamation of what I learned from them and what my clients, team members, and I have found useful.

Making Difficult Decisions Based on Your Values

Scarcity mindset can make us preoccupied with measuring up and doing things "just right." It can make us particularly fearful of criticism, judgment, and blame. Yet sometimes we have to make unpopular decisions that are rooted in our values and what we feel is right. I've found it's easier to be okay with judgment, criticism, and the disapproval of others when I feel steadfast in my choices.

For example, one of the most challenging decisions I've had to make at Girls Gone Strong is whether to provide educational resources about the topic of fat loss.

To understand why this decision is so challenging, here's some background: in the 1960s, the Health at Every Size (HAES) movement began advocating that the changing culture toward aesthetics and beauty standards had negative health and psychological repercussions for fat people. The movement has grown slowly since then and has picked up steam over the past thirteen years with Dr. Lindo (formerly Linda) Bacon's book, *Health at Every Size*, first published in 2008, and Evelyn Tribole and Elyse Resch's book *Intuitive Eating* (originally published in 1995, with the latest updated version published in 2012).

Both the HAES movement and intuitive eating approach are anti-intentional weight loss / fat loss because evidence suggests that most intentional weight loss efforts fail in the long term. They also argue that the yo-yo dieting that comes with intentional weight loss—along with the harassment, discrimination, weight bias, stigma, and lower-quality healthcare that people in larger bodies often experience—is more damaging than a person's weight.

As you might imagine, this idea has been paradigm shifting and, in some cases, polarizing. Some folks are 100 percent pro-HAES, pro-intuitive eating, and anti-intentional weight loss. Some folks believe that any person or organization sharing fat loss information is engaging in fat shaming, perpetuating anti-fat bias and stigma, and harming people in fat bodies.

On the other side of the spectrum, many people in the health and fitness industry roll their eyes at the HAES/intuitive eating community, insist that the "obesity epidemic" is what's causing our health crisis, and see it as their professional duty and personal mission to help millions of Americans lose weight and improve their health.

No matter which "side" you're on, people are angry at you and think you're part of the problem.

At some point, I had to decide: Would GGS discuss fat loss and give women options to pursue that goal? Or would we avoid the topic altogether?

Our team sat down together and considered our organizational values and how we could make the biggest, most positive difference. After much discussion and reflection, we came to a few conclusions.

Based on my many years as a coach and what I've seen and learned in the areas of behavior change, health coaching, and leadership, I believe that to make the biggest difference, you have to meet people where they are. We concluded that to help the most women, we had to speak to them about the issues and topics that matter to them—and for many women, that includes fat loss.

Further, from our perspective at GGS, the *most* empowering thing you can do for a woman is to honor her autonomy to make her own decisions about her body. We don't believe in limiting the goals women can have for themselves.

However, we recognize that a lot of women's weight-loss goals stem from unhealthy relationships with food and their bodies, social conditioning, internalized misogyny, harassment, discrimination, and so forth. (Basically, a lot of the limiting beliefs and systemic barriers mentioned in this book!)

We decided to commit to giving women the space to make whatever decisions they want with their bodies, while simultaneously working to cultivate an environment that:

- doesn't prioritize weight/fat loss over other goals
- displays a wide variety of shapes, sizes, ages, races, ability levels, gender identities, etc.
- shows women all the possibilities and potential goals for their lives and their bodies
- doesn't demonize or shame fatness (or any other body type)
- openly discusses the problems with fat phobia and fat stigma
- encourages women to move toward a place of body acceptance (and eventually embracement, if that's a goal of theirs)
- empowers women to choose what's right for them without shame or judgment

Additionally, plenty of companies are ready to prey on women's insecurities with quick fixes, fad diets, pills, powders, and gadgets. It was important to us that we help women make the healthiest and safest decisions they could within that context.

This decision-making process was exhausting and involved weeks of soul-searching—and the decision we landed on is up for continuous reflection and reevaluation. But knowing our values made it far easier and allowed me to find a kind of clarity I felt good about.

While some people applaud our approach, we also get a lot of backlash for it. Based on GGS's stance on this topic, I've even been told that we must "lack critical thinking skills"—despite having spent hundreds of hours researching and discussing it. I fully respect different viewpoints on this issue. But I also feel confident in the one we've chosen for ourselves, for now.

Here's another, simpler example of this kind of situation: A while ago, I met up with an old friend. We hadn't seen each other in a couple of years and were getting caught up. As part of "catching up" she began gossiping about some mutual acquaintances of ours. Gossiping about other people isn't aligned with my values, and it made me uncomfortable, so I stopped her and said, "Hey. I'm not super comfortable talking about other people like this. Tell me about what else is going on in your life."

In the moment it was awkward, but it would have felt worse if I hadn't spoken up and had engaged in an activity that's misaligned with what's important to me and how I want to be in the world. She was a little caught off guard, but totally cool about it, and the next time we hung out? No gossip.

Whether the circumstances are big or small, and whether they have to do with your personal or professional life, knowing your values is key. When you're clear on your values you can trust in your decisions, no matter what you're going through.

Strategy #2: Retrain Your Brain

As you define your values, you might start to see gaps between what's most important to you and how you're living your daily life.

For example, suppose kindness is one of your values. When you examine your daily actions, you might find yourself being kind *sometimes*. You also might notice yourself gossiping at work. Or mentally berating yourself and calling yourself names that are not very nice.

That is a disconnect between your values and your actions.

So what happens when you notice this discrepancy? You can shift your thought patterns and actions toward an alternative with a two-part strategy I call "reply and replace."

Part #1: Reply

Say you're scrolling through Instagram and see that a friend has posted a picture of herself in a swimsuit. Of the many things going on in the picture—the lush scenery, her smile, the beautiful wrap around her waist—your eyes are drawn straight to one thing: her flat stomach.

You feel a tinge of . . . you don't know what to call it. Jealousy? Bitterness? You start thinking about your stomach, which has always made you feel a little self-conscious. *I'd love to go on a vacation like that, but I could never go looking like this. I'd be too embarrassed to be seen in a bathing suit*, you think.

What do you do when you have that thought?

You pause, then ask yourself:

- Do I agree that having a flat stomach is what makes someone worthy?
- Is it true that I should only get to enjoy myself on a vacation if my stomach is flat?
- What would I say to someone I deeply love if she said she felt "not good enough" because her stomach didn't look a certain way?

Here's another hypothetical example. Imagine your colleague is newly single and her husband just moved out. Rumors swirl about what happened with her and her ex, and everyone is speculating about it.

Before jumping in with your own two cents, you might pause, then ask yourself:

- Do I want to be the kind of person who gossips about other women?
- Am I proud of my behavior in this moment?
- Does it align with my values to pass judgment on other people whose situation I don't know or understand?
- Is this how I would want someone to treat me if I were going through a difficult time?

Most likely, your answers to these questions will be some variation of no: *No, that isn't true. No, that's not how I want to be. No, that's not how I'd want someone to treat me.*

Part #2: Replace

Have you caught yourself in the midst of thoughts or actions that don't align with your values and that you don't agree with? Then it's time to replace that thought/action with something you *do* agree with.

To do this, I like to use these three exercises:

1. Ask, "What is the opposite of this thought?"
2. Ask, "What is the most generous assumption I can make of myself or someone else in this situation?"
3. Ask, "How can I shift this thought slightly to align with my values?"

Each of these exercises is a shortcut to a belief that is more accurate, helpful, and positive. Let's take a closer look at them.

Exercise #1: What Is the Opposite of This Thought?

Identifying the opposite thought will often take you straight to a more helpful belief. After all, the opposite of a negative belief is probably a more positive one!

Current Belief	Opposite Belief
I need to lose weight before I wear a bikini.	I don't need to have a certain body to wear a bikini.
I'm an impostor.	I'm smart and capable.
Nothing good ever happens to me.	There are many blessings in my life.
I'm not good at anything.	I have valuable skills and experience to offer.

Exercise #2: What Is the Most Generous Assumption I Can Make of Myself or Someone Else in This Situation?

This exercise is especially helpful when you find yourself judging another woman or feeling competitive with her in a negative way.

In the previous example where your neighbor's husband moved out, the most generous assumption you could make might be something like:

- *I'm sure she's doing the best she can given the challenging circumstances she's endured.*
- *I don't know what she's going through, but I hope she's doing well and taking care of herself.*
- *She's a resilient woman, and she'll make it through this.*

Trying to deliberately think new thoughts can feel weird at first. But our brains are built for this. This is a concept called *neuroplasticity*, which is your brain's ability to adapt and change over time.

Even so, it takes more time and energy to *create* a pathway than it does to *use* the same pathway once it's created. My therapist, Jaye Neal, once told me a great metaphor for this: Your brain's most used pathways are like the highway you've driven down a million times to get home. The path is smooth and well worn, and you don't have to put much energy or focus into knowing where to go or what to do. It's easy.

Creating new pathways is like off-roading through an unfamiliar field with tall grass in a four-wheeler. It's bumpy and requires a lot more focus and energy. It's more difficult than driving down the smooth highway, and you may be tempted to go back to the path of least resistance. But over time, if you're intentional about using this new path, you'll wear down the grass, the ride will become smoother, and you'll learn exactly where you're going. Eventually the ride will become easy. And the old smooth highway? That will become covered with grass and weeds, making it more difficult to use.

If you're finding it challenging to change your thoughts, no problem. You don't have to radically transform them overnight. That's where the third exercise comes into play.

Exercise #3: How Can I Shift This Thought Slightly to Align with My Values?

This is a great technique to use if you find the previous exercises a bit challenging. Every time you catch yourself thinking or saying something negative about your body, your abilities, another woman, etc., practice shifting your thoughts in stages.

STEP #1: Practice Shifting Your Thoughts from Negative to Slightly Negative

Negative. I hate looking in the mirror because I don't like my body.

Slightly Negative. Looking in the mirror is hard because I'm uncomfortable in my body.

STEP #2: Practice Shifting Your Thoughts from Slightly Negative to Neutral

Slightly Negative. Looking in the mirror is hard because I'm uncomfortable in my body.

Neutral. When I look in the mirror, I see my body.

STEP #3: Practice Shifting Your Thoughts from Neutral to Slightly Positive

Neutral. When I look in the mirror, I see my body.

Slightly Positive. When I look in the mirror, I see the body that has carried me through life.

STEP #4: Practice Shifting Your Thoughts from Slightly Positive to Positive

Slightly Positive. When I look in the mirror, I see the body that has carried me through life.

Positive. When I look in the mirror, I see the body that has carried me through life and done so much good for me, other people, and the world.

It's not always possible to shift your thoughts all the way from negative to positive, even with time. I've found that for most people, if you can at least get to neutral, you'll be in a much better place because the negative thoughts and emotions will no longer consume you.

As for me, I used this exercise to shift my perspective about the cellulite all over my legs. I used to see the cellulite and feel embarrassed or ashamed about it. It made me want to diet more and exercise harder and hide my legs until I deemed them good enough to be worthy of being seen.

Then one day I realized that was ridiculous. It dawned on me: my Gama had cellulite on her legs. My mom has cellulite on hers. My sister has it on hers. I have it on mine. And even when I got so lean that I lost my period and had well-defined abs, I still had cellulite on my legs.

If I waited until I no longer had cellulite on my legs to live my life and feel good in my skin, I'd be waiting forever.

So my exercise went something like this:

ORIGINAL THOUGHT: *Ugh. I have cellulite all over my legs. It's so embarrassing and makes me look out of shape.*

STEP #1: Negative to Slightly Negative

I'm uncomfortable wearing shorts because of the cellulite on my legs.

STEP #2: Slightly Negative to Neutral

I have cellulite on my legs and it's normal. Most women have cellulite, and even when I'm incredibly lean, it doesn't go away. So it has nothing to do with how fit or in shape I am or how worthy my legs are of being seen.

I haven't shifted my thoughts on this to a place of positivity, but that's okay. Now I see cellulite on the backs of my legs and have a neutral response. I know it's normal and has nothing to do with how valuable or worthy I am, what kind of shape I'm in, or how good of a coach I am.

Strategy #3: Curate Your Environment

As humans, we like to think we consciously control most of our choices. But the truth is that a large percentage of our thoughts and actions are a response to our environment.

Our environment has a huge impact on our daily behaviors. For example, if you have a bowl of fruit or a tray of your favorite veggies sitting on your counter throughout the day, you're significantly more likely to eat those fruits and veggies than if they were sitting in the bottom drawer of your refrigerator inside opaque Tupperware containers. Same with cookies. If you have a plate of cookies on your counter, you're significantly more likely to eat more cookies than if you kept them in a jar in your cupboard behind other food containers.

If your environment is filled with things (social media, traditional media, people, etc.) that don't align with your values and the type of person you want to be, you'll have more difficulty creating change in your life.

Fortunately, we have the opportunity to curate our environments. We can surround ourselves with the inputs that will encourage the outcomes we desire. And we can increase the likelihood of doing the things we want to do so we can be who we want to be.

Want a great place to start? Consider this: in 2019, humans spent an average of 142 minutes (2 hours and 22 minutes) on social media every day.[4] That's 72 hours a month. That means an easy way for most of us to start changing our environment is by curating our social media.

How to Curate Your Social Media

How the heck do you curate your social media so it is actively lifting you up and inspiring you, rather than making you feel like you're in a spiral of comparison, jealousy, and feeling bad about yourself all the damn time?

I've got you covered with a three-step process to follow:

1. Unfollow accounts that don't serve you.
2. Follow accounts that are more aligned with your values and goals.
3. Repeat the process with other media.

We'll take a closer look at each of these below.

Step #1: Unfollow Accounts That Don't Serve You

As you scroll through social media, anytime you feel yourself experiencing a twinge of jealousy, shame, comparison, or not-enoughness, unfollow the account that sparked those feelings.

The goal isn't to shield yourself from these sorts of images and ideas for the rest of your life. If you had to avoid every single thing that bothered you for the rest of your life, you wouldn't get to participate much in the world.

The long-term goal is to change your mindset. Ideally, you'll reach a point where fewer things cause negative feelings, and when things do upset you, you can choose how you respond. But part of that process is limiting the things that keep you feeling "less than."

Aim to unfollow a minimum of three accounts. If you find more to unfollow, great! You can continue pruning your social media to cultivate a healthier environment for yourself.

Step #2: Follow Accounts That Are More Aligned with Your Values and Goals

Curating your environment isn't just about what you remove. It's about what you *add*.

Your next task is to find new uplifting and positive social media accounts to follow, ones that leave you feeling happy and inspired. Here's a tip: I click on the profile of someone I love following or whose work I admire and see who *they* follow. This has helped me expand my network and social media circle and helped me discover incredible women I never knew about.

You can also search for accounts based on specific topics you're interested in. While you're at it, I highly suggest you seek to follow people who are different from you and who represent a wide range of identities and experiences—ages, races, genders, ethnicities, body shapes and sizes, geographic locations, abilities, sexual orientations, educational backgrounds, and more. The more you follow and learn from others, the more you'll widen your perspective, which is vital to helping you let go of old, limiting beliefs and bring in new, empowering points of view.

I recommend starting with a minimum of three. Over time, you'll continue to discover new, inspiring, informative accounts that align with your values.

Step #3: Repeat the Process with Other Media

Once you've unfollowed social media accounts that aren't serving you and started following social media accounts that align with your values, repeat steps 1 and 2 with other forms of media you consume on a regular basis, such as TV shows or movies, podcasts, books, magazines, etc.

Spotlight

These three women are creating spaces to help other women be themselves, claim their space, and love who they are.

» Jameela Jamil

Jameela Jamil knows many people want to change the world for the better—but it can be tough to know where to start when it comes to activism. That's where her online platform I Weigh comes in.[5]

In 2018, the British actor, radio presenter, model, writer, and activist started an Instagram account designed to be a safe and inclusive social media space where people can express their voices and share ideas, art, and stories that mobilize activism.

I Weigh has evolved into a platform that not only introduces folks to new activists and movements but also encourages listening and learning, teaching rather than punishing.

Jameela says, "We're going to change the culture. I want you to be able to come on I Weigh as a safe space on the internet where you can see someone who looks like you. And it's an allyship platform because I believe in progress, not perfection."[6]

I Weigh offers original content exploring a wide variety of social issues, including mental health, climate change, anti-fat bias and diet culture, and increasing representation of marginalized groups.

Through this powerful content, Jameela and her (so far) all female-run team believe they can combat harmful stereotypes and teach one another how to use our time and energy in a way that creates meaningful change in our communities and across the world.

In her words: "We're building a full activism platform to give young activists who don't have my privilege and my platform the chance and the access to be able to spread their word to the most important people."[7]

And it's working.

Jameela and I Weigh combined have several million people in their online communities, and as of mid-2020, I Weigh has been an integral part of changing global policies at Facebook and Instagram around diet and detox products being shown to minors. They're currently campaigning for two bills to reach the US Senate.

» Allison Tenney

As a former Division I and professional soccer player and current high performance movement and mindset coach, Allison Tenney is passionate about women and strength training. After years of working with women, she's on a mission to create cultural change that makes health and fitness more inclusive for everybody and every body. That was the driving force behind creating her in-person event, The Ignited Womxn Summit, in 2015.

The Ignited Womxn Summit is an annual event designed to teach women what wellness and leadership can mean through an inclusive lens. The goal is to work together to "actively dismantle limiting narratives and systems that no longer serve us" and the women around us.[8]

Through keynote presentations, panel discussions, and interactive work sessions, attendees get to learn more about "fitness, nutrition, and sustainable wellness solutions for women, as well as business strategy, goal setting, advocacy, and branding."[9]

Allison explained, "We're not afraid to tackle big topics like racism, sexism, ableism, etc. in the health and wellness world. These conversations create more opportunities for more women to share their stories and to be seen *and* heard. This is important because when we share our stories, we understand we're not alone, we value our individual differences, and we know we're stronger together."

The Ignited Womxn Summit shows how one event can have a lasting impact. (There's that powerful ripple effect again.) Allison said, "Many of the women are still connected, speak regularly to one another, have built lasting friendships, are collaborating on business projects, and feel supported to go after their dreams and desires. These women take what they learn and pay it forward ten times, like what you would never believe."

» Sonja R. Price Herbert

Sonja is a New York–based writer, speaker, classically trained Pilates instructor, and anti-racism educator. After being in the fitness industry for years, Sonja felt lonely in Pilates spaces, so she decided to do something about it.

In 2017, she started Black Girl Pilates, "a space specifically for and centered around Black women who teach Pilates to share ideas, successes, and struggles as instructors and teachers within the business of the method."[10]

The women of Black Girl Pilates, or BGPi as Sonja often calls it, also "identify and dismantle areas where Black women are left out, i.e., magazines, social media, conferences, trainings, etc. and confront those entities regarding the lack of Black women in these spaces."

In addition to being an online community, BGPi hosts regular in-person meetups and events.

To get an idea of the impact of something like Black Girl Pilates, consider this: Marimba Gold-Watts (also known as @articulatingbody on Instagram) won the 2018 Next Pilates Anytime Instructor Competition. She was the first Black woman to win that award and was heavily supported by Sonja and others in the Black Girl Pilates community.

Next Steps

In this chapter I provided lots of actionable tips to put into practice to help you live true to yourself. Below you'll find exercises to go along with each of the three strategies presented in this chapter:

» Discover your true values.
» Retrain your brain.
» Curate your environment.

The first exercise can be done immediately if you wish; the second two can be done over the next several days, while you continue to read this book. Alternatively, you can circle back to these exercises once you've finished the book or whenever it's right for you.

To download your resource guide, visit:
www.MollyGalbraith.com/book-resources

Exercise #1: Discover Your True Values

Getting clear on your value system helps you act in alignment with those values.

Step #1: Identify times in both your personal and professional life when you were the happiest.

- What were you doing?

____

____

- Who were you with? Were you alone?

____

____

- What other factors made you feel happy?

Step #2: Identify times you felt proud of yourself.

- Why were you proud?

- Were other people involved? If so, who?

- What other factors contributed to you being proud?

Step #3: Identify times you felt fulfilled and satisfied.

- What need or desire was fulfilled?

- How and why did this experience give your life meaning?

- What other factors contributed to your feelings of fulfillment?

Step #4: Identify times you felt most physically energized, at peace, or full of vitality and "flow."

- What were you doing?

- Who were you with? Were you alone?

- What else contributed to the feelings of energy, peace, and flow?

Step #5: Determine your top values based on your experiences of happiness, pride, fulfillment, and flow.

Review the list of common values below.

» accomplishment
» accountability
» accuracy
» achievement
» adaptability
» adventurousness
» altruism
» ambition
» assertiveness
» attentiveness
» awareness
» balance
» belonging
» boldness
» bravery
» calmness
» candidness
» certainty
» charity
» cleanliness
» commitment
» community
» compassion
» competence
» confidence
» connection
» consistency
» contentment
» contribution
» control
» conviction
» cooperation
» courage
» courtesy
» creativity
» credibility
» curiosity
» decisiveness
» dedication
» dependability
» determination
» devotion
» dignity
» discipline
» discovery
» diversity
» drive
» effectiveness
» efficiency
» empathy
» empowerment
» endurance
» enjoyment
» enthusiasm
» equality
» equity
» excellence
» experience
» exploration
» expressiveness
» fairness
» faith
» fearlessness

» ferociousness
» fidelity
» flexibility
» focus
» foresight
» fortitude
» freedom
» friendship
» fun
» generosity
» goodness
» grace
» gratitude
» greatness
» growth
» happiness
» health
» holiness
» honesty
» honor
» hope
» humility
» imagination
» improvement
» inclusivity
» independence
» individuality
» innovation
» inquisitiveness
» insight
» integrity
» intelligence
» intensity
» intuition
» irreverence
» joy
» justice
» kindness
» knowledge
» leadership
» legacy
» liberty
» logic
» love
» loyalty
» making a difference
» mastery
» motivation
» openness
» optimism
» order
» organization
» originality
» passion
» patience
» patriotism
» peace
» performance
» persistence
» playfulness
» power
» productivity
» professionalism
» prosperity
» purpose
» quality
» reason
» reliability
» resilience
» resourcefulness
» respect
» responsibility
» reverence
» risk
» security
» self-actualization
» self-reliance
» selflessness
» sensitivity
» serenity
» service
» significance
» simplicity
» sincerity
» solitude
» spirituality
» spontaneity
» stability
» status
» strength
» structure
» success

» support
» sustainability
» teamwork
» thankfulness
» thoroughness
» thoughtfulness
» timeliness
» tolerance
» transparency
» trust
» trustworthiness
» uniqueness
» unity
» usefulness
» vision
» vitality
» wealth
» wisdom

- Choose the twenty-five that resonate most with you.

- From the twenty-five, pare it down to ten.

- From ten, pare it down to five.

- From five, pare it down to your top three.

Step #6: Prioritize your values.

- Compare your first and second values and determine which is most important.

- Compare your second and third values and determine which is most important.

- Compare your first and third values to determine which is most important.

Step #7: Reality test your values.

- Would my closest friends, unprompted, say these were the values that mean the most to me?

- Would I support these values even if my choice was unpopular and put me in the minority?

- Am I prioritizing my work and my life according to these values today? If not, do I want to, and am I ready and willing to make the changes necessary to make this happen?

Step #8: Reaffirm your values.

- Do these values make you feel good about yourself?

- Are you proud of your top three values?

- Would you feel comfortable sharing your values with people you admire and respect?

Step #9: Envision putting your values into practice.

- Are there things you *think* on a regular basis that don't 100 percent align with your values? If so, what thoughts might be more aligned with your values?

- Are there things you *say* on a regular basis that don't 100 percent align with your values? If so, what might you say instead to ensure your words are more aligned with your values?

- Are there things you *do* on a regular basis that don't 100 percent align with your values? If so, what might you change about your actions to make them more aligned with your values?

Exercise #2: Retrain Your Brain

This exercise is similar to the one presented earlier in the chapter. But instead of coming up with the answers off the top of your head, this is an exercise you can do over time.

By practicing this exercise on an ongoing basis, you'll start to notice things you may not have paid attention to before—like times when you may be thinking, saying, or doing things that misalign with your values. Then you can use these exercises to shift your thoughts, words, and actions.

1. What have you *thought* this week that doesn't align with your values? How can you reframe that thought to be more aligned with your values?

If you aren't sure, ask yourself:

- What is the opposite of this thought?
- What is the most generous assumption I can make of myself or someone else in this situation?
- How can I shift this thought slightly to align with my values?

2. What have you *said* this week that doesn't align with your values? How can you change what you said to be more aligned with your values?

If you aren't sure, ask yourself:

- What is the opposite of what I said?
- What is the most generous assumption I can make of myself or someone else in this situation?
- How can I shift my words slightly to align with my values?

3. What have you *done* this week (or avoided doing this week) that doesn't align with your values? How can you adjust your actions to be more aligned with your values?

If you aren't sure, ask yourself:

- What is the opposite of this action or behavior?
- What is the most generous assumption I can make of myself or someone else in this situation?
- How can I shift my actions slightly to align with my values?

Exercise #3: Curate Your Environment

This exercise is about removing barriers and making it easier for you to shift the way you think, speak, and behave to better align with your values.

Please note that not every question may apply to you.

1. What three social media accounts are you choosing to unfollow because you feel worse after you view them?

2. What three social media accounts are you choosing to follow because you feel inspired and uplifted by them?

3. What three TV shows or movies are you no longer watching because you feel worse after watching them?

4. What three TV shows or movies are you choosing to watch because you feel inspired and uplifted by them?

5. What three books or podcasts are you choosing to stop consuming because you feel worse after you read or listen to them?

6. What three books or podcasts are you choosing to consume because you feel inspired and uplifted by them?

CHAPTER 6

Better Together

Treat other women like your sisters instead of rivals.

—JEN HATMAKER

CHAPTER 6

Better Together

In 2011, seven different women traveled to Cincinnati.

Alli came from Baltimore.* Nia came from Tennessee. Julia came from outside Chicago. Jen came from Las Vegas. I drove up from Kentucky. And Marianne boarded a plane from Northern Ireland.

We *thought* we were all headed to support Julia at her powerlifting meet and have a group workout. We had no idea what else was in store for us.

As planned, we kicked the weekend off with a workout. Just minutes into our warm-up, I could feel the positive energy in the room.

We squatted. We deadlifted. We pulled ourselves up over bars. We did push-ups and one-arm push-ups, and we pushed one another across the parking lot on sleds. We clapped and cheered and coached one another. It didn't matter if we were squatting 80 pounds or 280 pounds—we were so dang happy for one another.

The next day at the powerlifting meet brought more of the same—women patting one another on the back and high-fiving. No one was criticized or judged. No one looked shy or ashamed in their tight weightlifting singlet. The support was palpable.

And the noise! In addition to the clanking of barbells and heavy weights hitting the floor was the sound of women cheering at the tops of their lungs. They whooped and called out to friends and fellow competitors: "You got this!" and "Go, go, go!" and "Yes!"

Following the powerlifting meet, we spent the rest of the weekend hanging out, eating tons of food, and talking about our desire to help women discover their strength.

---

* Neghar, also from Baltimore, joined us at the second GGS meetup in November 2011, as mentioned in chapter 1.

By the end of the weekend, I felt a spark inside me. I'd seen what a room full of women supporting one another looked like, and I knew: I never wanted to go back.

I wasn't the only one riding high on the supportive vibes. The days that followed were a flurry of calls and messages among the group, discussing how we could turn our passion into a new platform to "preach the gospel" of strength training for women. Ultimately, we decided to start with a Facebook page, and we came up with the name: Girls Gone Strong.

The weekend had ignited our collective passion to help other women discover their physical, mental, and emotional strength. Sure, we were all pursuing this mission on our own, to some degree. We each had our own initiatives and projects: some women were bloggers, others were creating training programs, others (like me) were running their own gyms. And while all of that stuff was pretty cool, something was missing. We wanted to make a bigger difference, a greater impact. We wanted to connect more deeply and authentically with other women. We wanted to get out from our computer screens and daily routines and collaborate.

We didn't know what was coming next, but I had a feeling that as much as we could accomplish individually, we were definitely better together.

Better Together

Since that powerlifting meet and my work with Girls Gone Strong, I've stopped seeing other women as a kind of mirror for everything I'm not. Instead, I've come to embrace the idea that we are "better together"—and it's changed my life. From growing my business to surviving the loss of my dad to healing my body image to writing this book, I couldn't have done it without the unwavering support of other women.

I promise you: whatever you want to create in the world, whatever life you want for yourself, you're more likely to make it happen if you're willing to work with other women, rather than go it alone.

Here's what this looks like in practice:

Scarcity Mindset	Better Together Mindset
Putting off vacation or sick days for fear other women will get further ahead or take an opportunity from you.	Resting when you need it and enjoying your time off because you know the other women in your life have your back.
Not wanting to ask other women for help.	Feeling comfortable asking for help when you need it.
Stressing over trying to "keep up" or "do better" than other women.	Striving to do your best work and supporting other women in doing their best work, too.
Gossiping, criticizing, or cutting other women down.	Talking up and celebrating other women, knowing they do the same for you.
Avoiding teamwork or collaborative projects (or preferring to work with 'the guys').	Collaborating with other women knowing you can accomplish more together.

Imagine how much more we could accomplish and how much better life would be if we all chose to operate from the "better together" side of things.

This change is possible. *If* we choose to work together, we can make our collective impact bigger, not smaller.

The "Better Together" Approach

To truly be "better together" and put this mindset into action (at this point you know I love action) you must do four critical things:

1. Overcome self-doubt.
2. Believe in women's abilities.
3. Set and uphold your boundaries.
4. Forgive yourself and others.

Let's take a look at these one by one.

Critical Thing #1: Overcome Self-Doubt

You know how this goes by now, right? Before we can take the necessary steps to believe in and collaborate with other women, we have to get ourselves right first.

The foundation of better together is believing in women and their talents and abilities, and that has to start with believing in yourself. You must feel confident about your own abilities before you can feel comfortable and confident working with others.

If you're insecure in your own knowledge and abilities:

- you'll feel threatened by other women more easily
- you'll allow your ideas to be shot down or dismissed more quickly
- you won't have the confidence to speak up and challenge other people's ideas

These are all key pieces of the better together approach, and you won't be able to master them unless you believe in what you bring to the table.

> If you've ever doubted yourself, your worth, or your validity, believe me—you are not alone.

I hear stories like this from women all the time: whether due to their size and shape or education, age, experience, background, you name it—they doubt themselves. In fact, a recent study of college students found that women judge their own behavior more harshly than men do, underestimating their own potential.[1]

You might think that judging yourself harshly leads to better outcomes, and you might even consider this behavior a source of motivation. But self-doubt can have debilitating consequences. It can prevent you from going after the things you want in life, from pursuing the career or promotion or sport or opportunity. It can prevent you from standing up for your values and being the role model you want to be for the other women and the girls in your life. It can make you feel less confident, more uncertain, and generally less capable than you are.

Here's a five-step process you can use to work through self-doubt:

Step #1: Notice, Name, and Normalize

As discussed in earlier chapters, the first step to retraining your brain is becoming aware of the thoughts you want to change. If you've been doubting yourself for years, you may not even notice when these thoughts arise because they seem normal (and they are). But in order to change them, you must notice, name, and normalize them.

Self-doubt might sound something like this:

- I don't feel qualified to do this.
- People are going to find out that I don't know what I'm doing.
- I'm just not cut out for this parenting stuff.
- I don't want to speak up. What if people don't like my idea?

If these kinds of thoughts sound familiar, you may be struggling with self-doubt. The good news is that you can overcome it. And (bonus!), remember that naming how we're feeling also reduces the intensity of the emotion, so if your self-doubt makes you feel nervous, anxious, or unqualified, naming how you're feeling can help soothe that emotion and make the next step easier.

Step #2: Retrain Your Brain

You learned about retraining your brain in the previous chapter, and those same techniques can be applied here.

When you're struggling with self-doubt, you can retrain your brain by asking the following questions:

- What is the opposite of this thought?
- What is the most generous assumption I can make of myself in this situation?
- How can I shift this thought slightly to align with who I want to be?

Let's work through this example: *I don't want to speak up. What if people don't like my idea?*

- What is the opposite of this thought? *I can't wait to speak up. People are going to love my idea.*
- What is the most generous self-assumption to make? *I've put a lot of thought into this idea and I know it's good. I can handle it if people don't like it.*
- How can this thought be shifted just slightly? *I'm hesitant to speak up but I'm going to do it anyway. I'll be disappointed if people don't like my idea, but it will be great if they do.*

Step #3: Record Your Accomplishments and Compliments

Have you ever crushed a work assignment, received praise from your boss, and felt really good about yourself—only to have a single piece of negative feedback or criticism devastate you?

Part of the reason for this is negativity bias. *Negativity bias* refers to our proclivity to "attend to, learn from, and use negative information far more than positive information."[2] In other words, we focus on and remember negative events more than positive ones.[3]

That means you can accomplish ten amazing things, but if you struggle with one thing, your brain will hone in on that, which is why it's crucial to record your accomplishments and compliments and review them when you're trying to overcome self-doubt.

When you're feeling down and doubting yourself, reviewing a list of things you've done well and/or positive feedback you've received can help bring you back to reality and remind you of your unique abilities and talents.

You can start a journal for this, create a folder in your inbox, or use the notes app on your phone. Whatever method you prefer, make sure it's accessible when you need it most.

Step #4: "Train the Brave"

I first heard this mantra from author and expert in leadership, communication, and courage building Margie Warrell. When I feel fear or self-doubt, I ask myself: *What would I do right now if I were being brave?*

I used to think "brave" was a natural tendency—either you are brave, or you aren't. But over the years I've learned that bravery and courage are skills that can be learned and honed.

As with any other new skill, you can start small. For example, you can practice:

- speaking up (asking a question during a meeting or setting a boundary with a loved one)
- saying yes to a project that will stretch your abilities or put you out of your comfort zone
- making a challenging decision that aligns with your values but that others may disagree with

These kinds of victories will help you "train the brave," develop more self-efficacy, and practice overcoming self-doubt.

Step #5: See Outcomes as Data

Perfectionism—the drive to set our standards for ourselves impossibly high—can keep us stuck in self-doubt.

Did you know some studies suggest that women tend to struggle with perfectionism more than men?[4] According to psychologist and GGS curriculum developer Dr. Lisa Lewis, "perfectionism not only ruins the enjoyment of achieving goals, it is also associated with low self-esteem, and with women in particular, it's correlated with feelings of inadequacy."[5]

That may not surprise you. You might consider yourself a perfectionist or see these tendencies among the women in your life.

While at a glance perfectionism might seem like a positive driver, it can actually prevent you from reaching your goals.

Fortunately, you can use a powerful technique to move away from it.

The idea is to see outcomes as data. In other words, if you make a mistake, disappoint yourself, or otherwise fall flat on your butt, think of these things as data—information about what happened—rather than failure. If we can view all outcomes as data, rather than judgments about our own worth, it's easier for us to overcome self-doubt, make decisions, and take risks because we recognize that in all situations, we win or we learn (sometimes both).

The best reframe I've found for viewing outcomes as data comes from researcher Beck Tench, via habit expert James Clear. Beck recommends treating perceived failures the way a scientist would.[6] Scientists know that when they develop a hypothesis and run an experiment, various outcomes can occur, and all of those outcomes are points of data.

Scientists understand if they conduct an experiment and their hypothesis is proven wrong that it doesn't make them bad scientists. It simply provides them with more data they can use to guide future experiments. Every outcome, including your perceived failures, is a point of data you can use to help make better decisions in the future.

Critical Thing #2: Believe in Women's Abilities

If you've ever felt like your expertise or ideas weren't as valued as men's knowledge or opinions, it's not just you. Women's expertise and experience is often approached with more suspicion, doubt, and criticism than men's.

My good friend Rachel Balkovec knows this all too well.

Rachel was the first woman to hold a full-time strength and conditioning position in Major League Baseball with the St. Louis Cardinals in 2014, and in November 2019 she became the first woman hired as a full-time hitting coach by a Major League organization, the New York Yankees.

But blazing this trail wasn't easy.

When she first applied for full-time jobs in baseball, she got nearly no response, despite her incredible résumé.

By age twenty-four she had already completed six internships at legendary facilities like EXOS, Louisiana State University, and Arizona State University and had a short stint as a strength and conditioning coach for a St. Louis Cardinals affiliate, where she won the Appalachian League's strength coach of the year award. On top of that, she had experience playing Division 1 softball in college. And yet, she was having no luck in her job search.

Finally one team contacted her for an interview. It went great, and she was even told by the hiring manager she was "unofficially hired," and he'd be in touch the next day.

She didn't hear from him.

She was taken aback by this and followed up with calls and emails. After three weeks of silence, he called her with shocking news. He apologized and said he was told by his superiors that he wasn't allowed to hire her. And when he tried to send her résumé to other Major League organizations with open positions, he was met with the same response: *they weren't willing to hire a woman.*

Rachel was shocked.

This blatant gender discrimination meant she had to sit out a year of baseball and waitress to make ends meet, while taking on more internships to further bulletproof her résumé.

The next season when jobs started to come open, she wasn't taking any chances. She changed her first name on her résumé and applications to "Rae" and removed all gender-specific language.

Immediately the emails started pouring in, and the phone started ringing. And as soon as they learned Rae was a woman, she never heard from them again.

She continued to have the same struggles and planned to sit out the 2014 season as well. Thankfully, the St. Louis Cardinals remembered what a kick-ass intern she was and called just before spring training to offer her a job as the Minor League Strength and Conditioning Coordinator, overseeing ten male strength coaches and managing two hundred athletes on their way to the big leagues. She interviewed and got the job. The rest is history.

If you, like Rachel, have ever been disbelieved or doubted, I just want to say: it's not fair, and it's not your fault. Women are doubted all the time. And bias about things like race, class, sex, age, physical or neurological ability, and more, further influence how much we are believed or trusted by others.

The real kicker? Women aren't just doubted by men. We doubt *each other.*

The 2019 *Reykjavik Index for Leadership* (dedicated to measuring how men and women are viewed in terms of their suitability for leadership) found that only 59 percent of women in the United States would feel "very comfortable" with a female president. Only 66 percent said they'd be "very comfortable" if a female CEO led a major company. (Unsurprisingly, men were even less comfortable with women in these leadership positions.)[7] The data suggests that even women are holding other women back by doubting their abilities, particularly in critical leadership roles. If one-third of American women still aren't comfortable with a woman as CEO of a major corporation, think about how often women are being held back, unfairly judged, and scrutinized—not because of their talents or abilities but because of their gender (not to mention the layering of other biases related to intersectional facets like race, sexual orientation, and so on).

It's not just an absence of doubt and bias that women need: it's advocacy. We need people who will champion our ideas, help us get heard, campaign for us, connect us, and bang the boardroom tables in support of us. For many men, this kind of support helps them climb the ranks of their industry, get their projects the green light, or otherwise make progress in their lives and careers. Women need this too, and if we don't believe in them and their abilities and make a deliberate effort to champion them, they won't get it.

Fortunately, this is where you can make a difference: if we as women start believing in one another, we can help one another grow and succeed and create more opportunities—not just in work but in all aspects of our lives.

To start practicing this, you can adapt some of the techniques you used to overcome self-doubt:

Step #1: Notice and Name When You Find Yourself Doubting Women

If you catch yourself disbelieving, doubting, or making assumptions about another woman, pause and take notice. Noticing and naming the pattern is the first step to changing it. (You'll find an exercise in the "Next Steps" section that will help you notice and reflect on your assumptions and biases in more detail.)

Step #2: Retrain Your Brain

If you have a doubting, critical, or skeptical thought, stop and ask yourself:

- What is the opposite of this thought?
- What is the most generous assumption I can make of the person in this situation?
- How can I shift this thought slightly to align with who I want to be?

Step #3: Record Other Women's Accomplishments

With this technique, you'll expand on the practice of recording your own accomplishments to note other women's accomplishments.

This list may include women family members, friends, and colleagues but also may include women you see on social media, hear about in the news, or learn about through studying history. Aim to fill this list with women who have different backgrounds and experiences than yours.

Step #4: Check Your Biases

As I shared above, we all have biases, and the first step to overcoming them is to recognize them. At the end of this chapter I share specific ways you can tune in to what biases you may have for or against people, to ensure you aren't unfairly questioning, scrutinizing, or doubting women's abilities because they're women.

Critical Thing #3: Set and Uphold Your Boundaries

Boundary setting might sound selfish, but it allows you to be incredibly generous with your assumptions—because you don't allow yourself to be taken advantage of and you have a clear idea of what's okay and what's not okay. When we have that sense of security, we have more room to give to others.

When respected, boundaries also deepen trust. They give both parties clarity. There's no guessing in the relationship. These benefits allow us to work more collaboratively and constructively with others.

Yet as women, the struggle to prioritize our own needs and boundaries—and not feel bad or guilty about it—is *real.* This may be, at least in part, because women are typically praised for being devoted and selfless and for putting everyone else's needs before their own.

Boundaries are a huge topic that could easily take up their own chapter (or book!), but for the purposes of this section, here's what you need to know.

As stated above, boundaries are what you determine is okay and not okay in a relationship. Different experts categorize boundaries differently. I like to break boundaries down into six types:

- *Emotional:* boundaries around inappropriate topics, when it's okay to share and not share things, and dismissing, criticizing, or minimizing of emotions
- *Intellectual:* boundaries that give you freedom around your own thoughts, ideas, beliefs, and opinions
- *Time/energy:* boundaries around time, when and how it's okay to contact someone, favors or demands on time, and free labor
- *Material:* boundaries around money and possessions, specifically what you will share, with whom, and how your possessions are treated
- *Physical:* boundaries around personal space and touch, including what's appropriate in different settings, and unwanted comments regarding appearance or sexuality
- *Sexual:* boundaries include the emotional, intellectual, and physical aspects of sexuality, including consent, agreement, respect, understanding of preferences and desires, and privacy

You will likely need to set different boundaries with different people based on your relationship dynamic.

No matter what your boundaries are, you must clearly communicate and enforce them in order to make them effective.

Here's a quick and simple guide for how to set and enforce boundaries:

STEP #1: Determine what behavior or treatment is okay and not okay with a specific person.

STEP #2: Clearly communicate that boundary to the other person, including

- Why you're setting the boundary. For example, you care about them and want to have clear expectations for the relationship.
- What will happen if they cannot respect the boundary. For example, you'll have to stop the conversation, you'll leave, you'll take a break from the relationship, etc.

STEP #3: Invite them to share their boundaries with you too.

STEP #4: Remember that you are only responsible for setting the boundary—you are not responsible for their reaction to your boundary.

STEP #5: If they violate the boundary, enforce the consequence (e.g., stop the conversation, leave, take a break from the relationship, etc.).

Whose Boundaries Aren't Being Respected?

While enforcing your own boundaries is important, it's critical to recognize that certain folks are less likely to have their boundaries respected. As much as we might try to enforce boundaries, we don't have control over how other people respond. Black women, Indigenous women, Women of Color, trans women, women with disabilities, pregnant women, and others may find that their boundaries are more often disregarded. (Consider, for example, the fact that Black women often receive unwanted hair touching, even when they've expressly told someone not to touch their hair. Or that pregnant women's bellies are frequently touched without permission.)

One way we can lift women up is to do our part to help ensure all women have their boundaries respected. Drawing on inspiration from powerful women I am lucky enough to call friends, here are some ways we can do that:

1. Role model what it looks like to uphold your own boundaries.

"I think the more we all speak up about our own boundaries, the more we normalize boundary setting for others. And when we develop the skills to speak up for ourselves, we can stand up for other people when they need it as well."
—Jessi Kneeland, speaker, writer, and life coach

2. Talk to other folks in your life (kids, friends, family, colleagues) about respecting boundaries.

"It is the right of every single person to have boundaries, but having your boundaries respected is a form of privilege. So we need to teach people not just how to set boundaries but how to respect other people's boundaries as well."
—Erica Smith, sex educator, speaker, writer

3. Speak up and support women whose boundaries aren't being respected.

"If someone says that they feel disrespected, be loud about it. Be loud about it in your own way, but be loud about it. And hold that safe space so that person can express their boundary. Be a witness. Tell them, 'I've got you. You say what you need to say; I will be a witness for you in this situation.'" —Dr. Uchenna "UC" Ossai, pelvic health physiotherapist, professor, and sex counselor

4. Acknowledge the impact when another woman's boundaries are disrespected.

"When a woman tells you her boundaries are being disrespected, trying to brush it off with, 'Oh, well, that kind of sucks, but that's not really a big deal. Don't let that ruin your day,' minimizes the impact. Fully embrace the fact that if she's bringing it up, it's a big deal for her. Acknowledge its importance and help her feel heard and respected." —Carolina Belmares, fitness and nutrition coach, doula, and GGS curriculum developer

5. Respect other people's boundaries, especially if you're in a position of power.

"We must be vigilant about not encroaching on other women's boundaries. This is especially important for women who've been in their careers longer. There are often power dynamics in the workplace that make it harder for younger, newer women to have their boundaries respected. If we can respect their boundaries, that can make a big difference in their lives and workplace experience." —Kaniah Whitehorn Konkoly-Thege, attorney and corporate general counsel

Critical Thing #4: Forgive Yourself and Others

Holding ourselves accountable to do better requires an ability to keep moving forward—not holding grudges or getting caught up in the noise or in self-flagellation. As Dr. Maya Angelou famously said, "I did then what I knew how to do. Now that I know better, I do better."[8]

My dad taught me some valuable lessons about forgiveness. Given his cannabis campaign platform, he often was incredibly unpopular, even ostracized.

He and his ideas were ignored, laughed at, and criticized (and even though today they're becoming mainstream, he still hasn't been given the credit he deserves). But he had no time for holding grudges, complaining, or criticizing others; he was too focused on his mission.

A lot of people had negative things to say about my dad over the years, and at times it would make me really angry, but Dad didn't let it get him down. One day I asked him why he never got mad when people said mean things about him, and he said: "Baby, it's not what they call you. It's what you answer to that counts."

He knew who he was and what he was fighting for, and that's what ultimately mattered to him. Part of me feels frustrated that he died before he got to see so many of his ideas come to fruition, but then I remember another thing he said to me when other people were getting the glory for his hard work: "I don't care who scores the touchdown as long as my team wins the game."

In my early twenties, he showed me an even more profound picture of what forgiveness can look like. I don't know what the prompt was, but some sort of lightbulb went off in his head and he decided forgiveness was *everything*. Not one to sit on his ideas, he picked up the phone and, one by one, called the people in his life. He forgave them for mistakes they'd made and asked them to forgive him for his own.

I remember that he called his mother (my grandmother Dollie), and asked her forgiveness for all he had put her through as a difficult child and teenager and young adult. And he told her he forgave her for all of the things she did as a parent that he felt were difficult or flawed. (Of course, I'm not necessarily recommending this method. Other politicians weren't exactly thrilled with him calling them up and forgiving them for things they didn't think needed forgiveness.)

My dad used to say that forgiving someone is like taking rocks out of your knapsack: it leaves you feeling a lot lighter. That grudge that you might hold against someone else isn't renting space in your brain. Forgiveness makes you happier and frees up mental and emotional capacity. It allows you to let go and focus on living your best life and helping other people live theirs.

Forgiveness is often a challenging process, and I acknowledge that sometimes we experience incredibly difficult and devastating things at the hands of others. I can't speak to everyone's journey in forgiveness, but I do know that forgiveness doesn't mean condoning what other people have done. It does mean choosing to grant ourselves the freedom to let go and move forward.

Here are four powerful strategies I've used to "flex my forgiveness muscle":

1. *I Remind Myself That Forgiveness Is About Me, Not the Other Person.* It's about choosing to be free myself. When you recognize that forgiving someone is not about condoning their actions or letting them off the hook but rather about allowing yourself to live your fullest and happiest life, forgiveness becomes a bit easier.

2. *I Remember the Ways I Have Hurt Others.* I know my actions have caused other people immense pain at different times in my life, sometimes unintentionally and sometimes because I was selfish or careless with their feelings. This allows me to be empathetic to the other person's situation and makes forgiveness easier.

3. *I Recognize That Forgiveness Is a Skill.* Like other skills, forgiveness can be learned. Sure, it requires practice, and you won't always be successful, but you can get better. I've found that starting by forgiving small transgressions is key.

4. *I Reflect and Get Clarity on My Goals.* I want to lift women up, change the world, and live a full and happy life doing work I'm proud of. Carrying around resentment is antithetical to those goals. It wastes precious time, energy, and mental capacity. It keeps me from doing my best work. And it doesn't feel good. When I'm angry and struggling to forgive someone, I revisit my goals and remember that forgiveness actually gets me closer to where and who I want to be in the world.

What "Better Together" Is *Not* About

It's important to be clear that doing better together doesn't mean you have a responsibility to be friends with everyone, agree with everyone, like everyone, or be liked by everyone. As women, we often feel the need to be peacemakers, to be agreeable and not make waves. But you're entitled to hold your own opinions, to be disliked, and to disagree with others.

When you're working on the concepts in this chapter, keep the following in mind.

You Don't Have to Be Friends with Everyone

You might be reading this book because you're searching for deeper, more meaningful connections and relationships with other women—and I hope this book helps you do that. But it's impossible to have deep, connected relationships with a ton of people. Your emotional capacity is limited, and time is your most precious nonrenewable resource. Prioritizing how you spend your time is critical. Understand that you'll probably have a handful of very close friends, then a slightly wider circle of people you're pretty close with, then progressively wider circles of friends, colleagues, peers, and acquaintances, all the way out to strangers.

Your values and personality won't align with everyone. That's fine. You can still believe in the power of lifting other women up without trying to fit two puzzle pieces together that don't align.

The best advice I can give is to be intentional about how you spend your precious time and energy—spend it on people who fill you up and actions that help you live your values.

You Don't Have to Agree with Everyone

I think it's a great thing when we disagree with other people because this allows for important dialogue, critical thinking, and moving ideas and concepts forward. One tenet of how we work at GGS is that anyone on our team is encouraged to challenge anyone else on our team at any time. It's always done in a respectful way, and I cannot tell you how many times our work has become better because someone stood up and said, in one way or another, "No, I don't agree with that, or "This doesn't look right to me."

Of course, we must have a baseline level of agreement about the value of human beings and their worthiness as well as general levels of kindness and regard for other people. If someone doesn't agree that all people are worth kindness and respect, I don't have much time for that person. But we don't have to agree with everyone about everything all the time in order to lift women up.

Robert Jones Jr. probably said it best: "We can disagree and still love each other unless your disagreement is rooted in my oppression and denial of my humanity and right to exist."[9]

You Don't Have to Be Liked by Everyone

I understand the impulse to want to be liked by everyone. Who doesn't like to be liked? The problem is that it's impossible to be liked by everyone. And trying to be liked by everyone is a quick path to inauthenticity, misery, and, I would argue, business or career failure too.

Here's another secret: you don't have to like everyone either. Even so, you can still believe in their worth, want good things for them, want to see them succeed, and maybe even help them succeed in some capacity if that opportunity arises.

It's Not About Winning

In today's sociopolitical environment—with "cancel culture" and people being called out all over the place (sometimes for good reason)—it can feel like there's no winning, like you can't do anything right.

But in my opinion, life isn't about winning; it's about figuring out how you can continually do better. This whole idea about "winning"—winning the debate or the social media war or the argument—is misguided. It's a short-term, self-focused strategy where the objective is, well, to win. And that doesn't always serve the greater good or honor the real difference we can make in the world.

To me, "doing better" includes listening to people's perspectives, appreciating their lived experiences, and living according to my values. And it means recognizing that we are better together.

It also means taking small, daily action in service of lifting one another up. And that's exactly what you're going to learn about in the next chapter.

Next Steps

In this chapter I gave you lots of actionable strategies—including four critical things to do—to help you begin putting the "better together" motto into practice. Below you'll find the exercises that walk you through each of the four critical things introduced in this chapter:

» overcoming self-doubt
» believing in women's abilities
» setting and upholding your boundaries
» forgiving yourself and others

Some of the exercises can be done immediately, whereas others can be done as the opportunities arise and as you continue to read. You can also return to these exercises once you've finished the book or whenever it's right for you.

To download your resource guide, visit:
www.MollyGalbraith.com/book-resources

Exercise #1: Overcoming Self-Doubt

The next time you find yourself experiencing self-doubt or thinking you're not qualified to do something, follow these steps:

Step #1: Notice, Name, and Normalize. Write down the thoughts and feelings you're having and remind yourself they're normal.

Step #2: Retrain Your Brain. Ask yourself the following questions and record the answers to any or all of them:

- What is the opposite of this thought?
- What is the most generous assumption I can make of myself in this situation?
- How can I shift this thought slightly to align with my values?

Step #3: Record Your Accomplishments and Compliments. Recall at least two or three things you've accomplished or compliments you've received lately. I highly recommend putting them in a place where they're accessible so you can review them when you need them most, whether that's a journal you carry in your bag, a folder in your inbox, or the notes app on your phone.

Step #4: "Train the Brave." Next time you find yourself wanting to do something but feeling afraid—e.g., speaking up in a meeting, setting a clear boundary, making a hard decision, etc.—ask yourself: *What would I do right now if I were being brave?* And make a list of as many things as you can think of. Start with the smallest one and do it.

Step #5: See outcomes as data. Picture something you worked really hard on that didn't go the way you wanted—e.g., work project, room renovation, family trip, etc. Take a minute to write down how you felt when that happened, while reminding yourself it didn't make you a "bad" person/parent/teacher/employee/boss. Then take a moment to write down what you learned from the experience, and what you'd do differently next time.

Exercise #2: Believing in Women's Abilities

The first step toward believing in women is to check our assumptions and biases, but in order to do that, we must practice getting introspective.

Here's a method to help you do that.

1. Think of a woman you don't know well—e.g., someone you just started working with or a friend of a friend you recently met.

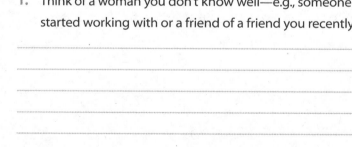

2. Ask yourself what assumptions you might be making (good or bad) about this woman's:

- Financial status
- Believability or trustworthiness
- Physical ability or disability
- Religious beliefs
- Occupation
- Relationship status
- Age
- Intelligence
- Sexuality

____

____

____

____

____

____

You might not be able to identify all of your assumptions off the top of your head, but it's good practice to start watching out for them. Once you're aware of your assumptions, you can notice if you're making unfair, negative assumptions about other women and begin challenging those assumptions.

Exercise #3: Setting and Upholding Your Boundaries

As mentioned earlier, boundaries are a much bigger conversation than can be covered in this chapter. For this exercise, think of one person in your personal or professional life you want to set boundaries with.

1. Who do you want to set boundaries with, and what behavior would you like to say is okay or not okay?

2. Why are you setting this boundary, and what will the consequences be if the other person cannot respect it?

3. When do you plan to share this boundary with the other person? Name the date, time, and location, and spend three minutes visualizing the scenario and practicing what you'll do if they react poorly or violate your boundary. This process will help you feel more prepared to respond appropriately if needed.

4. Can you think of a time you've witnessed another woman not having her boundaries respected? If so, what happened? What did you do? What might you do differently in the future, if anything?

Exercise #4: Forgiving Yourself and Others

The goal of this exercise is to provide some critical thought around forgiveness to help open your brain to new ways of thinking about it. To do this exercise, think of one person in your personal or professional life you want to forgive.

1. Who do you want to forgive, and what did that person do that you feel requires forgiveness?

2. Have you ever done anything similar to what that person did to you? If so, describe it.

3. How would it benefit you to forgive that person?

4. How does it benefit you *not* to forgive that person—e.g., holding a grudge feels good, not forgiving allows you to feel self-righteous, etc.?

5. What is holding you back from forgiving that person?

6. How might you feel or how might your life be different if you forgive that person?

CHAPTER 7

Taking Small, Daily Action

Real change is practically invisible as it's happening.

—MARIE FORLEO

CHAPTER 7

Taking Small, Daily Action

In my seventeen years working in health and fitness coaching, one sure thing I've learned is this: small actions add up.

In fact, almost anything we achieve—whether it's a big thing or a small thing—is the result of small efforts we take each day.

Think about it: on average, you probably spend four minutes per day brushing your teeth—two minutes in the morning and two minutes in the evening.

Four minutes is less than 0.3 percent of your entire day. Yes, that's less than one third of 1 percent of your day. It's almost nothing. But if you skipped that four minutes of brushing every day for a year, there's a good chance you'd end up with plaque, gingivitis, swollen gums, and multiple cavities.

Keep not brushing your teeth and a few years later you may be looking at crowns and root canals. Give it another ten-plus years and you could be getting dental implants or dentures.

Unpleasant to think about, but powerful, right? A mere four minutes a day spent brushing our teeth can lead to drastically different outcomes that impact our health, confidence, happiness, self-image, relationships, and bank account.

With our coaching clients, I've seen the same massive impact of small daily action. This is precisely what creates change over the long haul. A few minutes a day spent chopping up veggies and leaving them on the counter or standing up from the computer and stretching or going for a walk or doing a ten-minute strength-training session—performed consistently over days, weeks, months, and years—adds up to life-changing results.

The key to implementing new habits or actions into your life is to start small—so small you feel confident you can implement them with no problem. Starting small ensures you'll do the behavior and allows you to stack up habits and rack up "wins" that fuel you to keep going.

Lifting women up is a habit, pure and simple. Like any other type of habit, it's best practiced on a regular basis. I don't carve out hours of my week, every week, to perform huge acts of generosity toward other women. Rather, lifting women up in my life is more a series of small, regular acts that I often do without even thinking about them—kind of like brushing my teeth.

When you take small but regular action, you build momentum and gain practice with your new habits. You develop courage and self-trust as you do things you haven't done before. And you cast a powerful vote in favor of the person you want to be, all while lifting other women up along the way.

Your small actions can have exponential impact.

Imagine that one week you did something to lift up two women in your life, and those women were so inspired by you that the next week they chose to lift up two women in their lives. And the next week, those women chose to lift up two women. Within just ten weeks, 2,046 women would have been lifted up by other women. All from that one small effort you made.

This is where the ripple effect, which you learned about in chapter 3, takes hold. Every small action you make cascades, giving more and more women an opportunity to be lifted up and to lift up others.

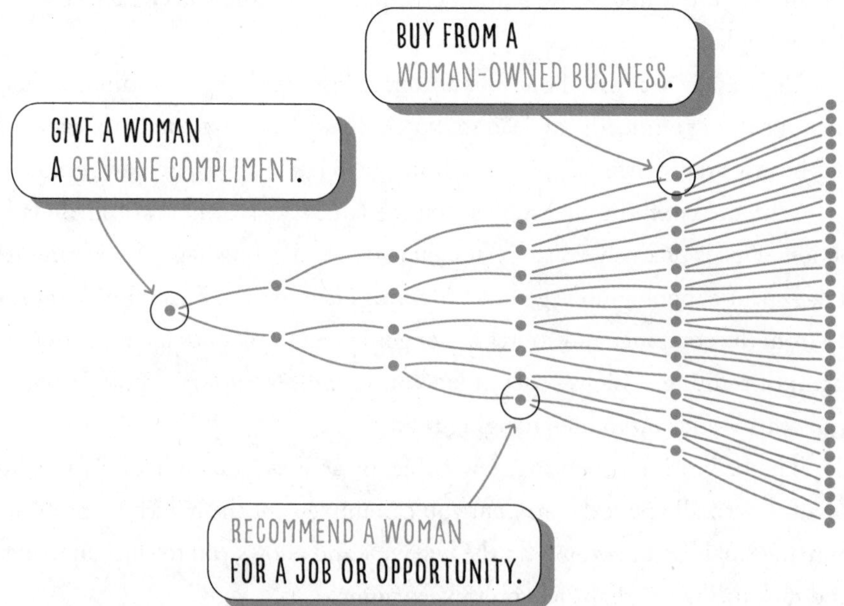

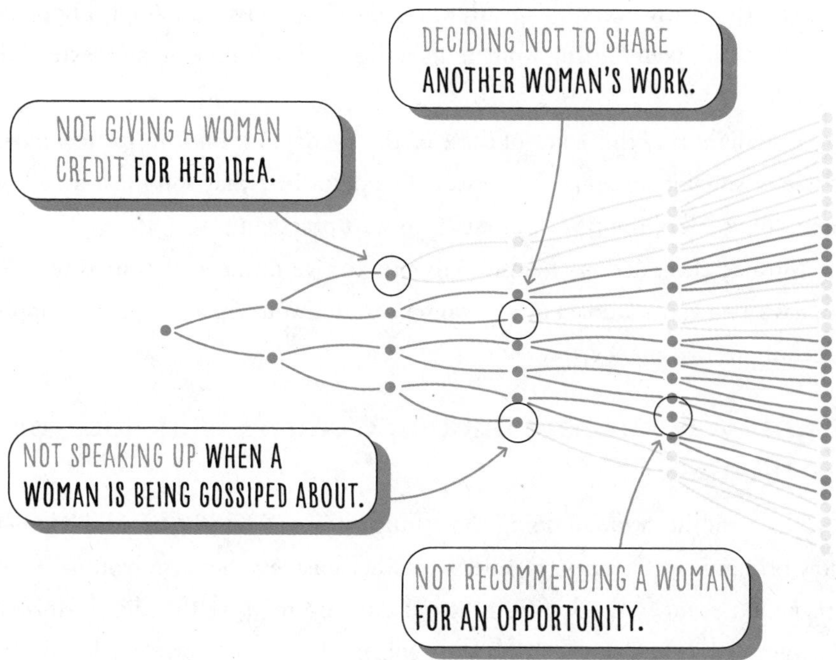

And the actions you don't take—well, those can break the ripple effect, as seen here.

In this chapter, you'll discover how many opportunities you have each day, week, and month to intentionally lift other women up. You'll see that it doesn't require much time, energy, or thought to make a big difference. We have countless ways to support other women, and the great news is, we can all participate.

You don't need to wait until the time is right or you have the "perfect" opportunity. You can start right now. Here's how.

Eight Small but Mighty Ways You Can Lift Women Up

Ready to take some small but meaningful action? Let's get to it.

These are by no means the only ways you can make a difference—and in the coming chapters we're going to explore some even bigger ways you can make an impact. For now, I'm sharing these particular tactics because they're accessible to nearly everyone, nearly every day. They give you ample opportunity to practice your "lifting women up" skills, and they don't require extensive resources.

You might find that some of these tactics overlap. Or some might feel more doable or suitable for you. No worries. The point isn't that you must do all of these things, all of the time, but rather to start practicing.

Most of these actions require only one to five minutes of your time and can have a powerful impact on the women around you while triggering a ripple effect of positive change.

Mighty Way #1: Share Another Woman's Work, Idea, or Creation

If you see another woman doing something awesome, tell the world! Help her show off (and get attention for) her work, her business, her art—you name it. I make it a point to do this on a regular basis on my social media platforms, whether it's a funny meme, a podcast episode I love, or a product I think is valuable. When I see women doing awesome stuff, I pass it on.

HOW SHARING CAN BENEFIT OTHER WOMEN:

- Raises awareness of them and/or their work
- Increases sales of their products or services
- Helps them gain new followers, fans, or community members
- Increases their reputation or success within their workplace or industry
- Helps their ideas gain support and traction
- Helps them gain new opportunities (e.g., speaking gigs, job offers, collaborations, etc.)
- Helps them feel valued and supported

Share Another Woman's Work, Idea, or Creation	» If you discover a product you love from a woman-owned business, tell your friends and family about it. » Share another woman's profile or work on social media and explain what you like about her or her work (be as specific as possible). Tag her in the post so others can find and follow her easily. » If your colleague has a great idea, share it with your peers or your boss (giving your coworker credit, of course). If the idea has already been shared, champion the idea to help it gain support and traction from the team.*

*In the world of getting stuff done and creating new solutions, ideas don't get resources without people championing them. If more women champion the ideas of other women, then more resources will be allocated to them.

Mighty Way #2: Give Another Woman a Genuine Compliment

Do you ever feel like no matter how much you're juggling, or how hard you're trying, your efforts somehow aren't good enough? Like you always have to hustle to prove your worth or keep doing better and better?

This is a product of scarcity mindset. For many women, enoughness feels just out of reach. I hear this often from women in the Girls Gone Strong community: as women, we feel like we always need to be better looking, better parents, better employees/bosses, better caretakers, or better neighbors—you name it, we feel we need to improve. To be clear, wanting to get better is great. Feeling like you're never enough is not.

Giving a genuine compliment to another woman is a powerful antidote to this scarcity. Sure, the idea of giving a compliment might seem incredibly simple. But it matters. A compliment, thoughtfully given, can benefit the recipient in many ways. It can boost her confidence, mood, and attitude. It can help her recognize her unique abilities (the things she's so great at that she takes them for granted). It can encourage her to keep striving despite the obstacles. And it can inspire her to pass the kindness on to other women.

That's a lot of good from just a few words.

Feeling pumped to tell your friend how beautiful she is? Hold up.

Earlier in the book I talked about how, as women, there's disproportionate focus on our bodies; folks of all genders routinely judge, scrutinize, compare, and focus on women's bodies. Complimenting women on their looks reinforces all that. Instead, I recommend complimenting women on qualities that have nothing to do with their appearance—like effort, skill, drive, compassion, intelligence, professionalism, and so forth.

Another caveat: if you have a close relationship with another woman and have her permission to comment on her body, you certainly can—but ideally you'd compliment her on things much more important than how she looks.

Here's a list of meaningful compliments you can give women that have nothing to do with their appearance:

- You always have my back.
- Your passion inspires me.
- You're so creative. I love how your brain works.
- You make me want to be a better person. I'm glad we're friends.
- I have so much respect for you and your work.
- You're really funny.
- I admire your compassion for other people.
- You're a great listener. I always feel heard by you.
- You bring out the best in people.
- You're a great leader. I really enjoy working for you.
- I'm inspired by your confidence and willingness to put yourself out there.

If you still find that your instinct is to compliment women on their appearance, I get it. I, too, catch myself opening my mouth to comment on other women's bodies from time to time, then my brain catches up to my mouth and

I promptly shut it. With practice, you'll find it easier to compliment women on the amazing things about them that have nothing to do with what they look like. And your words will make a positive impact.

HOW GIVING COMPLIMENTS CAN BENEFIT OTHER WOMEN:

- Improves their confidence and self-efficacy
- Helps them recognize and use their strengths
- Inspires them to support other women
- Helps them feel valued and supported

Mighty Way #3: Catch Another Woman Doing Something Right

Remember that negativity bias we talked about in the last chapter? How we as humans tend to focus on things that go wrong, or things we do wrong?[1]

I like to flip the script here and practice catching women doing something right. Catching women doing something right flips all this negativity on its head.* It involves keeping an eye out for women who are doing a good job with something and acknowledging it. That "something right" might come from a barista who put the extra bit of care into your latte or your boss who made a difficult but important decision or your sister who disciplined her child with grace.

Whatever the case, notice the good thing she's doing, and extend your appreciation. A simple, "Hey Abby! Good job with _____," can go a long way. (But I have more ideas for you below!)

By the way, catching a woman doing something right is similar to paying a compliment but a bit different. I consider a compliment to be related directly to who the individual is as a human, while catching a woman doing something right focuses more on a specific action, situation, or behavior.

* The concept of "catching people doing something right" is something I learned from Dr. John Berardi and my friends at Precision Nutrition. It's also well described in the book *Essentialism* by Greg McKeown.

HOW CATCHING ANOTHER WOMAN DOING SOMETHING RIGHT CAN BENEFIT HER:

- Increases her reputation or success within her workplace or industry (if shared with a coworker or boss)
- Improves her confidence and self-efficacy
- Helps her recognize and use her strengths
- Inspires her to support other women
- Helps her feel valued and supported

Catch Another Woman Doing Something Right	» Email your coworker and tell her how great she did in your team meeting. Be specific in your feedback about what she did well. Share how prepared she was, how confident she seemed, how thoughtfully she discussed an important topic, or how well she handled feedback from your boss. » Next time you're at a restaurant or store and getting great service, ask to speak to the manager and praise your server or sales clerk. Be specific. Is she patient in answering your questions, polite when your child is misbehaving, or knowledgeable about the products or menu? » Tell someone you're interacting with that she's doing a good job. It could be a friend, family member, colleague, gym buddy, service provider—anyone. You can tell the grocery clerk or post office employee they're nice to talk to. Or you could leave a positive comment on someone's social media or send them a direct message (DM).

Mighty Way #4: Give a Woman Credit Where Credit Is Due

Have you ever been in a meeting and made a suggestion that was generally ignored? Your colleagues don't say much or they skip to the next subject. A few minutes go by, and a guy in the room suggests the exact same thing—and this time, he's applauded for his brilliance.

Men get credit for women's ideas. All. The. Time. There's even a term for this: *hepeating*. Hepeating happens when a woman suggests an idea and it's ignored, then a guy says the same thing and everyone loves it.[2]

Unfortunately, women—especially women of marginalized groups—are chronically undercredited.

Making sure other women get due credit might seem like a small thing (especially if you haven't experienced it personally) but it matters a lot. It's not about looking good or showing off; getting credit for your ideas, work projects, creations, quotations, and contributions helps you build trust, social capital, relationships, reputation, and more. Credit is often an essential currency for climbing the ladder at work, building a business, getting elected, getting hired, and more. That's why it's so important to give women—particular women of marginalized groups—credit for what they do and contribute. This can be done in public, in front of coworkers, bosses, friends, family, on social media, in published material . . . wherever these conversations take place.

Spotlight

» Who Got Credit for #metoo?

Women of marginalized groups are often undercredited for their contributions. Together we can help change this.

Consider the game-changing "me too" movement. Tarana

Burke founded the movement in 2006. The organization was born of Tarana's own experiences with sexual violence and her time as a youth worker. In the early years they "developed [their] vision to bring resources, support, and pathways to healing where none existed before."[3]

In October 2017, in the days following the sexual harassment and assault allegations leveled against Hollywood producer Harvey Weinstein, Alyssa Milano spoke up about her own experience with sexual assault. She posted a tweet asking her followers to respond with "me too" if they'd ever been sexually harassed or assaulted. The #metoo wave took over social media as people began telling their stories.

According to the "me too" movement's LinkedIn page, "In less than six months, because of the viral #metoo hashtag, a vital conversation about sexual violence has been thrust into the national dialogue. What started as local grassroots work has expanded to reach a global community of survivors from all walks of life and helped to de-stigmatize the act of surviving by highlighting the breadth and impact of a sexual violence worldwide."[4]

While Milano's intent was to support victims of abuse and assault, many people (including high-profile media) assumed that she'd created this hashtag and movement and incorrectly credited her for it. Meanwhile, Tarana Burke—who'd started the movement over a decade before—wasn't initially acknowledged by the media. To many, this oversight was another example of Women of Color not receiving the credit or support they're due.

When these concerns were raised, Alyssa Milano stated she'd

been unaware of the preexisting campaign and its phrasing and then took steps to credit Tarana Burke in a *Good Morning America* interview. Since then, Alyssa and Tarana have appeared on multiple media outlets together and have individually and collectively raised a great deal of awareness about an issue that had been swept under the rug for years.

The moral of the story: we must be vigilant about making sure women, and especially women of marginalized groups, get credit for their work.

HOW GIVING A WOMAN CREDIT WHERE IT'S DUE CAN BENEFIT HER:

- Raises awareness of her and/or her work
- Increases sales of her products or services
- Helps her gain new followers, fans, or community members
- Increases her reputation or success within her workplace or industry
- Helps her ideas gain support and traction
- Improves her confidence and self-efficacy
- Helps her recognize and use her strengths
- Inspires her to support other women
- Helps her feel valued and supported
- And perhaps most of all: helps her gain new opportunities—e.g., speaking gigs, job offers, collaborations, etc.

Give a Woman Credit Where Credit Is Due	» In a meeting, if you notice a female colleague isn't getting credit for an idea or solution she came up with, mention it in the meeting. When another coworker talks about the idea, you can say, "Yes! I was excited to hear Grace bring that up. I think it's a great solution that will help us achieve our goals." » If you see a social media page using a quote or sharing work from someone else and not crediting her, leave a comment crediting the person whose work is being shared. It could be as simple as, "I love this quote! I believe it belongs to @Amber125. You should tag her in this post so she gets credit." » If you know a woman worked hard pulling together a big project—the football banquet, a school supply drive, the Girl Scout sleepover, a fundraiser—reach out to her and thank her for her work and make sure others involved know how much effort she put into the project to make it a success.

Mighty Way #5: Be Intentional in Your Spending

My gym used to be right next door to an awesome local woman-owned café called Coffee Times in Lexington, Kentucky. The owner, Terri Wood, has been running the business for nearly forty years, and all the staff have worked there a long time. Coffee Times is not only dedicated to serving great coffee (they have their own roasting plant in the back of the shop), but the ambience is warm and inviting, and the staff always remember your name and order.

I don't own the gym anymore, but I still drive out of my way to go there or have their decaf cinnamon nut graham coffee shipped to me when I'm traveling. Yes, I love their coffee. But I especially love supporting a woman-owned business.

I've come to learn that spending money is like voting with your dollars. When you put your money toward the kind of businesses or products you want to see in the world, you increase the likelihood that they—and others like them—will be able to thrive. As the late entrepreneur and activist Leila Janah said, "budgets are values in action."[5]

Using your dollars to support women-run businesses is important. More women are starting their own businesses than ever before, but evidence suggests that on average, women-owned businesses grow at a slower rate and earn less revenue than businesses owned by men for three reasons:

- "Few role models and a lack of mentors that contribute to the perception that entrepreneurship is a male-only endeavor [*and* it contributes to a lack of insider knowledge and access to powerful networks];
- A gender pay gap that hurts the ability of women to be successful entrepreneurs;
- Unequal access to startup funding and financing streams that leaves women with fewer credit options and a small portion of venture capital."[6]

You can help change that, simply by spending your dollars with them.

By helping a woman-owned business thrive, you're helping not only the business owner(s) but also the other women they interact with. For example, if they hire women, you're helping those women get jobs. If they buy from women-owned suppliers, you're helping those businesses succeed too. If the company makes charitable contributions or "gives back," you're helping them increase their impact. Plus, you're helping the business owners serve as powerful role models, further inspiring, mentoring, or role modeling entrepreneurship for other girls and women. Talk about a powerful ripple effect!

The best part is you don't have to spend a lot of money to make a big impact. If you're on a tight budget, think less about *how much* you're spending and more about *where* you're spending. When and if you have a chance to make a buying decision, aim to be more deliberate about where that money is going.

One important note: supporting women-owned businesses doesn't mean supporting any and all woman-owned businesses. If a business isn't doing a good job—if its products aren't high quality or its customer service is subpar—then it's not doing you *or* the business any good to spend your money there. Give constructive criticism if the situation warrants it (for example, tell the manager if you have a poor customer service experience) and then move on.

HOW BEING INTENTIONAL WITH YOUR SPENDING BENEFITS WOMEN:

- Increases sales of their products or services
- Increases their reputation or success within their workplace or industry
- Helps them gain new opportunities (e.g., speaking gigs, job offers, collaborations, etc.)
- Improves their confidence and self-efficacy
- Inspires them to support other women
- Helps them feel valued and supported
- Again, perhaps most of all: helps them create new jobs and opportunities for women

Be Intentional in Your Spending	» If you have the choice between a big coffee chain or a local woman-owned business, buy your coffee from the woman-owned coffee shop to support her business. Same with event catering, wedding cakes, bodegas, food trucks, gift shops, art—you name it. » If you're looking to hire someone for a service (legal services, life insurance, house cleaning, financial planning, nutrition coaching, web design, etc.), when gathering trusted recommendations, ask folks if they know any women who provide these services, and do your due diligence to find the right provider for you. » When searching for a product or service online, include "woman-owned business" or "owned by women" in your search so you can find a list of businesses owned by women to choose from. » *Bonus:* Make sure you tip adequately when appropriate. A quick online search of whether tipping is customary in an industry can provide guidelines of what to tip. And if you can tip a little more, it's always appreciated. (Can you tell I waited tables and bartended for years?!)

Mighty Way #6: Endorse or Recommend Another Woman's Work

I always say that if I love someone's services, I'll become their biggest evangelist. What could be an easier way to support other women than being a raving fan?

What's the last women-owned business that you did business with? Did you write them an online review? Have you shared your experience with your friends or family?

Endorsing or recommending another woman's work has broad applications, spanning leaving someone a review on her Facebook business page to writing her a letter of recommendation or nominating her for an award or promotion.

Recommending or putting your stamp of approval on another woman's work goes a long way—probably further than you think. Word of mouth and personal recommendations are powerful drivers of business and success. Evidence indicates that word of mouth influences 59 to 91 percent of all purchases.[7] Research from Nielsen shows that 83 percent of people trust recommendations from friends and family.[8] And a 2019 consumer survey from BrightLocal found that 81 percent of people between the ages of eighteen and thirty-four trust reviews they find online.[9] Translation: your endorsement matters.

Plus, endorsing or recommending someone can help her build confidence in her own abilities. That combination of endorsement and confidence can help her break into male-dominated industries or teams that have a "boys' club" mentality.

As mentioned with spending, endorsing or recommending another woman's work doesn't mean endorsing or recommending *all* women's work. If you don't think she's doing a great job and you don't feel comfortable recommending her, then don't. This type of lifting women up only works when you're giving a genuine and authentic endorsement.

That said, if you don't want to endorse her, it's worth getting introspective and asking yourself why. Our internalized biases sometimes show up in our lack of belief in women's abilities, so make sure you take a moment to ask yourself: Is it her or you?

HOW ENDORSING OR RECOMMENDING ANOTHER WOMAN BENEFITS HER:

- Raises awareness of her and/or her work
- Increases sales of her products or services
- Helps her gain new followers, fans, or community members
- Increases her reputation or success within her workplace or industry
- Helps her ideas gain support and traction
- Helps her gain new opportunities (e.g., speaking gigs, job offers, collaborations, etc.)
- Improves her confidence and self-efficacy
- Helps her recognize and use her strengths
- Inspires her to support other women
- Helps her feel valued and supported

Endorse or Recommend Another Woman's Work	» Recommend a woman's work or product to a friend, family member, book club, or other group you're associated with. » Leave her a positive review on Google or Facebook. These reviews are incredibly powerful drivers of business. » Nominate her for an award, or write her a formal letter of recommendation for a job, promotion, committee, or graduate program.

Mighty Way #7: Speak Up When You Hear Something Negative Said About Another Woman

As you start tuning in to how people speak about other women, you'll likely notice a lot of negativity—judgments about her body, her clothing, her life choices, the way she parents, how she does her hair, the decisions she makes at work, or even the insidious: "I don't know. There's just something about her I don't like. I can't put my finger on it." (Notice that this is different from constructive criticism. This is unnecessary negative judgment, commentary, or gossip.)

The next time someone says something like that, speak up.

As someone who used to spend her life mired in gossip, I know how tempting it can be, and how good it can feel, to engage in gossip. Looking back now, I can see I engaged in negative gossip primarily when I was feeling bad about myself and/or when I was looking for a distraction from my own life. I also can see how harmful my behavior was to myself and other people. My gossiping not only kept me stuck in scarcity mindset but also hurt other women's reputations, broke their trust, and deteriorated friendships.

Here are three things you should know about speaking up.

First off, it can feel awkward, weird, scary, or all three of these things! Depending on the situation you're in and what's being said, it can be difficult to speak up—but you can do it. If you want, you can start small and with someone with whom you have a good relationship, where the stakes are low. (For example, speaking up to your best friend versus your boss). As we discussed in the previous chapter, you can "train the brave" and ask yourself: *What would I do if I were being brave in this situation?* Build your courage by getting more practice.

Second, speaking up can carry certain risks depending on the situation and the power dynamics around you. For example, if you're a boss in an organization and you hear something inappropriate, it certainly behooves you to speak up. But what if you're in a situation like the one Dr. Uchenna "UC" Ossai told me about? In her words:

> A friend of mine who's Black confided in me that her white boss told her to shut the F up in front of seven of her colleagues. She was new at the time. And

she didn't know anybody and she didn't know if any of her colleagues would protect her. So she didn't say anything in that moment; she walked away.

She says she doesn't regret how she handled it—not because of respectability politics, but because she felt it protected her emotional well-being at the time. That was the safest thing for her at that moment. She told me if that happened now, because she knows her colleagues better and feels confident they would have her back, she knows she'd feel much more comfortable asserting herself. And I get that. I've been in similar situations myself, and the power of knowing others will bear witness to your experience and support you can change everything.

With UC's story in mind, I can't tell you exactly when to speak up and when not to. That's a personal choice for you to make. But I can tell you that I want you to stay safe, *and* I want to challenge you to speak up for yourself when you can and back other women up whenever you can, even if it's outside of your comfort zone.

Third, despite the complexities, speaking up is really, really important. Speaking up when someone is saying something negative about another woman or treating her poorly can have a cascade of positive effects on the person speaking, the person being spoken about, and those observing the situation.

Here's how this plays out.

You Help the Person Being Spoken About

For instance, if an untrue rumor is being spread about a woman, you can stop it in its tracks and possibly prevent it from damaging her reputation.

In some cases, you might even be able to bolster her reputation. For example, "You're calling her abrasive and making it sound like she's over-the-top, but the truth is she's straightforward, prepared, gets things done, and holds everyone accountable to do their best work. That's hardly being over-the-top. I think she's one of the most qualified women I've worked with."

You Help the Person Speaking

The act of speaking negatively about others is so common and accepted that some folks don't even realize they're doing it. By speaking up, you're raising awareness about the problematic nature of what they said, and depending on what you say when you speak up, you may give them an opportunity to correct themselves, clear up any misunderstandings, or apologize.

You Help the Observers

By speaking up, you're modeling good behavior for others and possibly inspiring them to do the same the next time they're in a similar situation. Depending on the outcome, you may also help them see that speaking up can have a positive impact on everyone involved. Additionally, you could be building trust and strengthening your relationship with them (whether you know it or not) because they know you won't stand for negative gossip.

You Help Yourself

Speaking up can benefit the person being spoken about, the person speaking, and those observing, but it's good for you too. You get to "train the brave" and flex your bravery muscles. You also get to help other people, live your values, build your confidence, and have the peace and calm that comes with knowing you're living true to yourself.

HOW SPEAKING UP WHEN YOU HEAR SOMETHING NEGATIVE SAID ABOUT ANOTHER WOMAN BENEFITS HER:

- Increases her reputation or success within her workplace or industry (if you speak up and praise her in front of bosses, colleagues, or peers)
- Helps her ideas gain support and traction
- Helps her gain new opportunities (e.g., speaking gigs, job offers, collaborations, etc.)
- Improves her confidence and self-efficacy (if what you said gets back to her)
- Inspires her to support other women

Speak Up When You Hear Something Negative Said About Another Woman	» If someone makes an inappropriate joke or insinuation, ask them to explain it. Saying, "What exactly do you mean by that? I don't get it," often leads them to embarrassing themselves trying to explain what they said or realizing what they said isn't okay, dropping it, and apologizing. » Say, "That was a really unkind thing to say. Why would you say something like that?" and wait for them to answer. Maybe they didn't notice how unkind it was or maybe you misunderstood what they said. If so, this gives them a chance to explain. If not, and it was intended to be rude, sit in the awkward silence. If they play it off as a joke, follow up with, "Why is that funny?" Again, wait for them to answer. Don't let them try to shame you for speaking up. » Let the person know that what they are saying hasn't been your experience, and share what yours has been. You could say, "That's interesting. That's not been my experience with Keisha at all. I think she's smart, qualified, prepared, and great at her job. I enjoy working with her."

Mighty Way #8: Consider Calling Someone In

You probably know about being "called out," which is when someone says in front of other people that you've done something wrong. "Calling out" is like pointing your finger and yelling, "Hey, you really screwed up!" right in front of that person's family and friends.

"Calling in" is different. It's a calmer interaction where you bring an issue to someone's attention privately. It's saying, "Hey, I want to let you know you did this thing, and I feel like you could have done it better and here's why."

"Calling out" can get inflammatory quickly because of how our bodies are made. The second we're called out in public, our sympathetic nervous system (the "stress" system) goes into overdrive. When that stress system is in overdrive, we don't have room to take in new information and ideas. In that moment, our brain isn't primed for learning—it's primed for survival and defensiveness. That's why we start making excuses and justifications.

On the other hand, if we have a compassionate, one-on-one conversation, we're more likely to feel calm and safe, which is a lot more conducive to learning, growing, and doing better.

Just like speaking up, "calling in" helps everyone involved.

It Helps the Person You're Calling In

I wouldn't be where I am today without help from other women who lifted me up by calling me in, helping me see other perspectives, and encouraging me to do better. If we do this in a supportive way for one another, with the goal of doing better together, then we have a huge opportunity to learn and grow and get stronger.

When you call someone in, you're being generous. You're investing your precious time and emotional energy into someone else because you believe in them and their capacity to do better. If you didn't respect them, and believe in them and their ability to accept your constructive feedback and grow, you likely wouldn't waste your time calling them in.

It Helps People Who Aren't Present

When you call someone in, you're potentially minimizing harm for other people who might not be present. When you call someone in when they've done something harmful to others, whether it's sexist, racist, homophobic, transphobic, ageist, classist, or just plain cruel, you're helping decrease harm to others, particularly those in marginalized groups.

It Helps You

Like speaking up, calling in allows you to live your values and help other people at the same time. It can help you be the person you want to be, make the kind of difference you want to make, and work collaboratively to create the kind of world we all want to see.

> I use the following process to call someone in:
>
> » I share my concerns about calling them in, so my vulnerability helps lower their defenses.
>
> » I try to create a space where they know they are cared for and supported.
>
> » I try to help them see how they might have harmed me or someone else.
>
> » I explain that I know they aren't that kind of person and why I think they can do better.

Here's an example of how this process works. Suppose I overhear my coworker making a rude comment about one of our colleagues. I'd probably say something like:

> Hey! I have something I need to talk with you about. I'm a little concerned you might feel defensive when I share this, so first I want you to know that I don't think you were intentionally being harmful. I'm telling you because I care about you. Earlier today when you made that comment about Fabi—that was not okay. It's harmful because [insert reasoning here], and I don't think you're the kind of person who wants to hurt other people.

As you can see, calling someone in isn't about winning a fight or proving someone else wrong. It's about helping us all work together to do better.

A Critical Caveat About Calling In

I want to share an important consideration I've learned from a number of social justice educators: folks who are members of marginalized groups and experience oppression should not be expected to do the intense emotional labor of "calling in" folks who are oppressing them, particularly for free.

This means we shouldn't *expect* women to spend their time calling in men who are harming women with sexist jokes or dehumanizing language, or who brush off critical topics like the gender wage gap, unpaid domestic labor disparity between men and women, and the opportunity gap between men and women.

Same for Black, Indigenous, and Women of Color (BIWOC). For example, if a white woman is being harmful to BIWOC, it is not okay to expect BIWOC to experience that harm and create a "safe space" to educate that white woman on why she's being problematic. Same for LGBTQIA+ folks and other members of marginalized groups.

That said, there are plenty of members of marginalized groups who choose to "call folks in" for free, or even for a living. That's a personal choice. The point is that it is unfair to *expect* folks to do this work, and even worse, to *expect them to do it for free*.

If you're unfamiliar with issues related to marginalization and social justice (and/or find yourself getting called out or called in), I encourage you to do more learning about these topics.*

---

* To be clear, I'm not a social justice expert. To learn more, consider reading *I'm Still Here: Black Dignity in a World Made for Whiteness* by Austin Channing Brown, *Me and White Supremacy: Combat Racism, Change the World, and Become a Good Ancestor* by Layla F. Saad, and *So You Wanna Talk About Race* by Ijeoma Oluo.

HOW CALLING PEOPLE IN BENEFITS WOMEN:

- Increases their reputation or success within their workplace or industry (if they do better, they may have a chance to grow as leaders)
- Improves their confidence and self-efficacy (if they choose to grow and do better as a result of your feedback)
- Inspires them to support other women (if they take your words to heart and choose to do better)
- Bonus: minimizes harm / potentially prevents future damage

Consider Calling Someone In	» Say, "Earlier today when you made that joke, it wasn't funny. What you said is harmful to People of Color, and here's why [insert reasoning here]. I don't think you know this, which is why I'm sharing it with you now. I know you aren't trying to be hurtful, which means you can't say stuff like that." » Say, "I wanted to let you know that word is no longer appropriate to say. It's harmful to LGBTQIA+ folks. I know it can feel tricky to keep up with evolving language, but it's important because language shapes how we see the world and ultimately how other people are treated. The correct term for that is [insert term here]." » Say, "I wanted to reach out and let you know how much I enjoyed your conference this year, but I noticed there were only two women speaking out of ten presenters. I want to recommend three women who I think would be great speakers at your event next year. The first woman is [insert name here]."

Small Acts Snowball

Remember that you never, ever know how your small efforts may snowball. Let me give you an example.

In 2014, my former business partner and I invited two women—Sarah Fragoso and Dr. Brooke Kalanick—to speak at a conference we were hosting at our gym. Fast-forward a few years, and Sarah and Brooke invited me to be on their podcast, *The Sarah & Dr. Brooke Show.*

A few months after the podcast aired, I got an email from a physio and pre- and postnatal expert named Marika Hart. Marika reached out to share how much she enjoyed the podcast I did with Sarah and Brooke and told me to keep up the great work as she sent me a virtual high five from Australia.

I received that email from Marika at the exact time we were looking for a pre- and postnatal expert to help us at GGS. I emailed Marika back, hopped on a call with her, and invited her to start doing some work with Girls Gone Strong, including contributing to our coaching certifications.

Along the way, I had some questions related to our certification and getting it accredited in Australia. Marika said, "You must talk to this amazing woman. Her name is Mish Wright. She's been in the fitness industry in Australia for years advocating for women, and she knows how everything works."

Marika introduced me to Mish, who generously volunteered a couple hours of her time to help me navigate a difficult situation.

A few months later I got an email from Mish asking me to give the keynote presentation at her Women's Health & Fitness Summit in Melbourne, Australia—where I not only got to meet Marika in person and deepen our personal and professional relationship—but I told Mish I wanted to speak on the subject "Strong women lift each other up," and she gave it the green light.

After my talk, I was flooded with women generously sharing their compliments and appreciation. Because they were so passionate and authentic in sharing their enthusiasm for my talk, it gave me the confidence to turn my speech into a book. If they hadn't made the decision to get out of their seats, to come talk to me, to share their feedback, stories, and support, I might never have thought of writing this book.

To me, this experience shows the ripple effect of small actions in service of lifting other women up. If it weren't for the small but meaningful efforts of each of these women, this book would literally not exist.

You can have the same kind of impact. Never doubt how much your small efforts can add up.

Next Steps

In this chapter I shared eight small but mighty ways you can lift women up in your everyday life:

» Share another woman's work, idea, or creation.
» Give another woman a genuine compliment.
» Catch another woman doing something right.
» Give a woman credit where credit is due.
» Be intentional in your spending.
» Endorse or recommend another woman's work.
» Speak up when you hear something negative said about another woman.
» Consider calling someone in.

Nearly all of these strategies to lift women up can be done immediately in some way. I encourage you to start small, and focus on one strategy at a time. You can choose to focus on one strategy a day for ten days, or you can choose one strategy and practice it until it comes naturally to you and then move on to the next. You can also return to these exercises once you've finished the book or whenever it's right for you.

To download your resource guide, visit:
www.MollyGalbraith.com/book-resources

When you're ready to do the exercises, start keeping a record of the strategies you put into action for accountability, reflection, and inspiration. For each strategy, note each of the following:

- what you did
- who it was for
- how it felt
- what the result was (both immediate and medium- or long-term)

It can take a while to do all of these things. Don't rush to try to put them all into action at the same time. You can keep coming back to these exercises as often as you like.

Exercise #1: Share Another Woman's Work, Idea, or Creation

Exercise #2: Give Another Woman a Genuine Compliment

Bonus: Call a woman on the phone specifically to give her a genuine compliment (no other agenda). You won't believe what kind of magic can happen when you do this.

Exercise #3: Catch Another Woman Doing Something Right

Exercise #4: Give a Woman Credit Where Credit Is Due

Exercise #5: Be Intentional in Your Spending

Exercise #6: Endorse or Recommend Another Woman's Work

Exercise #7: Speak Up When You Hear Something Negative Said About Another Woman

Exercise #8: Consider Calling Someone In

CHAPTER 8

Your Voice Matters

I believe that telling our stories, first to ourselves and then to one another and the world, is a revolutionary act.

—JANET MOCK

CHAPTER 8

Your Voice Matters

Your story has power.

In 2012 and 2013, at the height of my struggle with body image, I was tired of how I felt about my body negatively affecting my self-worth. And I was sick of my abilities as a trainer being questioned because of how my body looked.

As I started to untangle my worth from how my body looked, a newfound sense of freedom began to emerge. It was incredible, and I couldn't keep it to myself. I wanted it for other women too.

Even though doing so felt terrifying and vulnerable, I needed to talk about my body image struggles. I needed to tell other women what I'd been through. And I needed to make a declaration: your worth does not—I repeat, *does not*—depend on the size of your thighs or whether you have visible abs or anything else you can think of.

After letting my ideas marinate for a while, I sat down and wrote a blog post called "It's Hard Out Here for a Fit Chick." The post discussed how even I, as a fitness professional who was supposed to "have it all together," struggled with body image, and how my profession led me to experience more scrutiny about my body, since many folks think trainers are supposed to "look the part" (whatever that means).

While talking about body image struggles may feel mainstream today, very few people were talking about it then and especially not health and fitness professionals. We were supposed to have it all together—our nutrition, our exercise, our mindset, our overall health. We weren't supposed to have, much less show, lumps or bumps or stretch marks or cellulite. We were supposed to be the poster children for "health," as defined by mainstream fitness magazines: low body fat, lightly muscled arms, six-pack abs, smooth legs (you know the drill).

With hands shaking and butterflies in my stomach, I hit publish on my website, shared the blog post on social media, started sweating a little bit, and then stepped away from the computer.

Well, that's that, I thought.

I put on my shoes and went for a walk with a friend. I figured that even if no one ever read the blog post, it felt good to speak my truth.

When I got home an hour later, the post already had hundreds of comments and shares and thousands of views.

In the next couple of days that number steadily increased to more than fifty thousand blog post views, and the comments and stories I received from other women were incredible. They saw themselves in my story, and my words helped them feel seen, heard, and known.

Sharing my story was a turning point for me and GGS, as it expanded my definition of "lifting women up" to include helping other women discover their freedom and body autonomy. As I worked through my own healing, I began sharing what I learned and saw the tangible impact my words, and my honesty, could have on other women dealing with the same struggles.

As I learned that day, and as you'll learn in this chapter, our voices are powerful.

By being honest and sharing our experiences, we can create a sense of connection and help women know they're not alone. We can also help women understand and contextualize their experiences. For example, as more women share their experiences with workplace harassment, other women realize they've been harassed, too, and didn't realize it before because the behavior was normalized in their workplace.

At a broader level, we can raise awareness about important topics and remove shame or stigma. As an example, I've heard from women that because I've been outspoken about going to both individual and couples' therapy, they've been inspired to seek therapy themselves.

Sharing our stories doesn't have to be all about difficult or depressing topics either. As you'll learn in this chapter, we can share the good news of our lives and inspire other women by showing them what's possible.

Speaking up didn't always come easily to me. As a young woman, I stayed quiet far too often. I was scared of displeasing other people and wanted to make everybody happy.

Fortunately, I've since embraced the power that our own voices can have. I've also learned that small acts of speaking up can have a massive positive impact.

You don't have to have a platform, ten thousand followers, or even a megaphone to make a difference. Your voice, your opinions, your stories—and your ability to help *other* women get their voices heard—are downright powerful.

In this chapter, I'll show exactly how to use your voice to lift yourself *and* other women up and how you can overcome anything that's standing in your way of speaking up and using your voice for good.

Spotlight

» Janae Marie Kroczaleski

In fitness circles, Janae Marie Kroczaleski is something of a legend due to her competitive accomplishments under the name Matt Kroc.*

Kroc was famous for being big, badass, and ridiculously strong. On April 25, 2009, Kroc set the male world record in the 220-pound weight class, with a 738-pound bench press, 810-pound deadlift, and 1,003-pound back squat. In addition, Kroc served in the Marines and provided security duty for President Bill Clinton. He was also super jacked.

"I was considered the ultimate alpha male."

What most people didn't know was that Kroc was transgender—something Janae has known since she was five years old.

* Janae identifies as transgender, gender fluid, and nonbinary. When speaking about the period of time during which she competed as "Matt," Janae uses he/him pronouns.

Over the years, Janae started carefully coming out to family and friends. But she was hesitant to come out completely due to fear of repercussions, especially for her three sons.

Then, in 2015, she was outed by a YouTube blogger.

After that, Janae made a decision. "If my story was going to be told, I wanted to be the one who told it."

Janae accepted interviews with outlets ranging from *Muscle & Fitness* to the Huffington Post, TMZ, and *Inside Edition*. Despite mixed results (sometimes outlets took a "sensationalized" approach), she embraced the opportunity to speak publicly and live fully "out" as her true self, Janae. In 2017, Janae was the subject of an award-winning documentary, *Transformer*. She is now a full-time motivational and educational speaker.

Interestingly, even with all of the mainstream media attention she's received, personal, honest conversations are perhaps what have helped Janae come into her own the most.

"I had two desires from a very young age: one was strength training and the other was that I was supposed to be female. But I was always taught to believe these two were opposing: we're conditioned to believe that men are big and strong and brave and competitive and aggressive, and women are supposed to be weak and mild. So growing up I was always wondering, *Why do I like strength training so much? But then why do I have all these feelings? And then how am I supposed to balance that? How am I supposed to figure that out?*"

When Janae first came out, she felt pressure to move away from strength training and lose all her strength and muscle. "Initially I dropped 72 pounds in four months; I went from 272 all the way down to 200. And I had planned to drop a lot further than that. Then I realized it was making me miserable. I thought, *I'm achieving this more 'feminine body.' Why does it not feel good?*"

Once she started opening up to women in the strength community, she realized her feelings were normal. "I discovered the women in the strength community had the exact same struggles I did. They had the desire to be bigger and stronger and got all this pushback from society and friends and family. All of that, 'Now you look like a man. That's not what women do. That's not very feminine' [stuff].

"Having these conversations really helped me to accept myself and accept that I'm a girl who likes to strength train and there's nothing wrong with that. I always say, 'Strength doesn't have a gender.' Now, in turn, I'm able to spread that message to other women who struggle with the same thing."

By sharing her story among family and friends, Janae has continued to see the impact of her honesty grow. As people in her life have become more supportive of other LGBTQIA+ people, the ripple effect of her story has continued to grow.

For example, Janae recalls, "One of my very close friends, his father-in-law came out as gay a few years after this. And it was really, really tough on the whole family. No one in the family supported him—except my buddy and his wife. They said the only reason they supported him was because of me."

These kinds of stories spur Janae to keep speaking up.

"I get private messages daily from people in the trans community, from trans women who felt like me, who were into strength training and didn't think they could ever transition, just thought it was never an option. And they say, 'You being open and honest about your story has given me hope to pursue becoming my true self.'

"When you hear stories like that and understand how other people's lives are being affected, how can you not share your story?"

What If Sharing Opens Me Up to Criticism, Or Worse?

I can guarantee you something: if you're sharing your story in a public way—such as on the web—other people will have something to say about it. And their opinions won't always be positive, kind, or legitimate.

If you avoid sharing your story because you're afraid people will judge you, know that they already *are* judging you.

In a way, knowing you'll be judged is kind of freeing. If you can accept in advance that speaking up will result in criticism, the inevitable criticism becomes easier to handle. You can then go ahead and do the brave thing. We all have two options.

Option #1. We can worry, play small, pretend to be someone we're not, and try to avoid judgment, which is futile.

Option #2. We can be authentic, speak our truth, share our story, and let the chips fall where they may.

I'm definitely in favor of the second option.

For extra credit, you can even think of potential rude or mean comments as a way to practice responding and modeling the kind of behavior you want to exemplify.

I have a four-step process I use to handle negative comments, which you also can use if it resonates with you:

STEP #1: RESPOND INSTEAD OF REACT. Pause before you do anything, which allows you to take a few deep breaths, think about the situation, and respond rationally, not emotionally.

STEP #2: CHECK IN WITH YOUR ENERGY. Do you have the mental and emotional capacity to respond right now? If not, then ignore the comment. If you do, then respond. For me, I also take a moment to recognize the privilege that comes with being able to opt in or out of conversations. I do this because I know my work is a marathon, not a sprint, and the reminder helps keep me from burning out.

STEP #3: CHECK IN WITH YOUR VALUES. Ask yourself if responding will align with your values. For instance, "making the biggest difference while doing the least harm" is my highest value. If I think my response can make a positive difference in some way, I'll do it.

STEP #4: GIVE PEOPLE THE BENEFIT OF THE DOUBT. Ask yourself, *What's the most kind and generous way I can respond to this person?* Then respond that way. This is less about letting people "off the hook" and more about me responding in a way that I feel proud of, and I feel most proud when I give other folks the same grace I would want.

I love this four-step process because it allows me to manage my emotional energy, stay aligned with my values, and treat people with kindness—even when doing so is tough.

Bringing your voice into the world can be intimidating. But you don't need to overcome your fears before you speak up.

As author Maggie Kuhn said, "Speak your mind—even if your voice shakes."[1]

All that said, I want to acknowledge that when it comes to speaking up, it's not always an even playing field. Some complex power dynamics play a role in terms of who gets to speak up, when, and how.

Take, for example, this story from GGS curriculum developer Carolina Belmares:

> I'm an immigrant. I was born and raised in Mexico, and I have been living in Canada for the past eleven years. A few years ago, there was a situation in which people were going to gather at the American consulate in Toronto to protest the treatment of immigrant families being separated from their children. That stuff hits me on a whole bunch of levels because I'm Hispanic, and I'm a mom and doula. I can honestly say my mental health was really suffering because the news hit me so hard. I felt desperately that there must be something that I could do, and donating money didn't feel like enough. So I thought, *I'm just going to go to the protest. I need to take action.*

And then I had a conversation with my social justice teacher Dr. Tee Williams. He was very clear with me that given the kind of immigration status I hold, I'm in a position of deep vulnerability and there could be really severe consequences for me. If anything in the protests turned in a way that was not purely peaceful, I could pay for it dearly—perhaps even with deportation.

So in the end, I had to make the decision to not go at all and not speak up for something that mattered to me very much because I would basically be jeopardizing my entire life and future with my children here in Canada.*

As Carolina's story shows, our particular experiences with oppression and vulnerability may mean that speaking up can be even more dangerous, risky, or harder to prioritize. This is all the more reason that, when we can, we *must* use our own voices to make it safer for other women to use theirs.

Spotlight

» Chrissy King

When coach and trainer Chrissy King started sharing fitness-related content online, she considered her articles and posts "good," but nothing out of the ordinary.

Her hesitation was partly due to stereotypes. "I was very cognizant of my identity as a Black woman. Historically, anytime I didn't agree with the dominant opinion, people would say, 'Oh you're just an angry Black woman.' So I was really, really careful to stay away

* Dr. Tee emphasized the importance of the most privileged folks stepping forward to prevent vulnerable people with the least privilege from having to risk severe harm. Further, he explained there are many ways to organize that don't involve protesting. In this case, Carolina's immigration status put her in a vulnerable position; thus, she chose to engage in other forms of activism.

from anything I thought would be controversial because I didn't want to be seen that way or have people think that about me."

But this carefully managed persona didn't fully align with Chrissy's true self.

"Online, I had this very vanilla personality. And it was fine. But outside of the online space, I was having conversations about race, feminism, and politics. And more and more it became hard for me to continue doing the work I was doing without talking about things that really mattered to me."

One day, she sat down and wrote an article.

"In the fitness industry, I didn't see a lot of representation of Black women or Women of Color in general, and I didn't see a lot of diversity in body types portrayed. It just seemed fitness was being marketed to very thin, privileged, white women who had access to money, as though fitness were only for those people. I knew that wasn't true—in my own life I saw other women who look like me working out. But I didn't see us represented anywhere, and I felt that was really missing." In response, she penned an article called "Is Fitness Only for Thin, White Women?"

After sitting on the article for some time, Chrissy got up the courage to publish it—a small, but brave act.

The article resonated powerfully with many women. "I got a lot of messages from Black women saying, 'Wow. Thank you for writing this article because it's something I've been feeling for a long time, but I didn't know how to put it into words.'"

After that, Chrissy started speaking up and writing candidly. She realized that if she wanted to make an impact, she had to get comfortable with negative feedback.

This led to a cascade of changes in her life, including leaving a corporate job she wasn't happy with. Amazingly, the more Chrissy continued to speak up, the more opportunities came her way:

paid speaking gigs, podcast interviews, and freelance writing for major magazines like *Shape*, *SELF*, and *Health* (and communities like Girls Gone Strong).

Chrissy's work now includes a solid online community, creating and selling her own training programs, virtual training and coaching, nonprofit work with Women's Strength Coalition in Brooklyn, hosting antiracism webinars for fitness and wellness professionals, and even partnering with a major organization to create an antiracism certification.

"I look at my life three years ago (before publishing the article), and it's like I don't even recognize that person anymore on so many levels. All those little things I did along the way led me to feel more confident and know that I can do this."

Meanwhile, she continues to hear directly from women who are lifted up by her writing.

"Every time I write something for Black women, in particular, I get messages about how it's been healing for them to celebrate their Blackness and to accept their bodies and to celebrate being a Black woman. Every time I get a message, I remember how important it is to keep saying these things and keep speaking up."

Beyond sharing your own story, there are some powerful ways you can use your voice to lift other women up and strengthen your sense of self. Let's take a look.

Share Your "Good News" Stories—And Celebrate Other Women's "Good News" Stories

Have you ever had really exciting news to share and felt like you had to keep it to yourself for fear that sharing it would come across as bragging? Or that your friends or loved ones would struggle to be genuinely happy for you? That they might judge you for sharing or assume your good news means everything in your life is perfect?

If you've ever experienced this, you know how awful it feels. Often women feel like we have to downplay our accomplishments or play small so we don't make other people feel bad.

What we don't realize is that sharing our successes and accomplishments can inspire other women to see what's possible for their lives.

While women are typically encouraged not to brag or think too highly of themselves, sharing what you love, what makes you happy, or what you're passionate about can have a positive ripple effect, helping women discover those things for themselves and, in turn, inspire others.

That was the premise of GGS when we started. We wanted to "preach the gospel of strength training" by sharing how it has positively impacted our lives. Since then, I've discovered that by talking openly about the good things in my life, I can give other women freedom to do the same.

By "good things" I mean things like:

- feeling good in my body
- liking myself
- choosing to *not* apologize for being different
- living my life as a happy, confident woman who is sure of herself and steadfast in her decisions (most of the time, anyway)

Even a single story of passion and enthusiasm can inspire other women. Here's an example of that ripple effect in action. Many moons ago, my good friend Neghar Fonooni (one of the cofounders of GGS) wrote a blog post on GGS about her experience with strength training.

A new trainer named Jennifer Vogelgesang Blake ("JVB") read the article, and Neghar inspired JVB to start seriously strength training herself.

Eventually, JVB became a powerlifter, and we featured her in a GGS spotlight on our website.

Shortly after, Chrissy King (yes, the same Chrissy you just read about!) was reading JVB's spotlight, and as a powerlifter herself, it encouraged her to reach out and connect with other women powerlifting—and even inspired *her* to become a coach too!

The simple sharing of these stories led to a cascade effect of all these awesome and influential women starting to lift, connecting with each other, and becoming coaches—and in turn they've now inspired so many more women to pursue their own strength.

At the same time, it's important to practice expressing (and feeling!) genuine joy and enthusiasm for other women's good news. The more we practice feeling genuine joy for other women when good things happen to them, the more comfortable they feel sharing their accomplishments and successes, and the more likely they are to speak and express genuine joy to and for other women. The ripple effect takes place again:

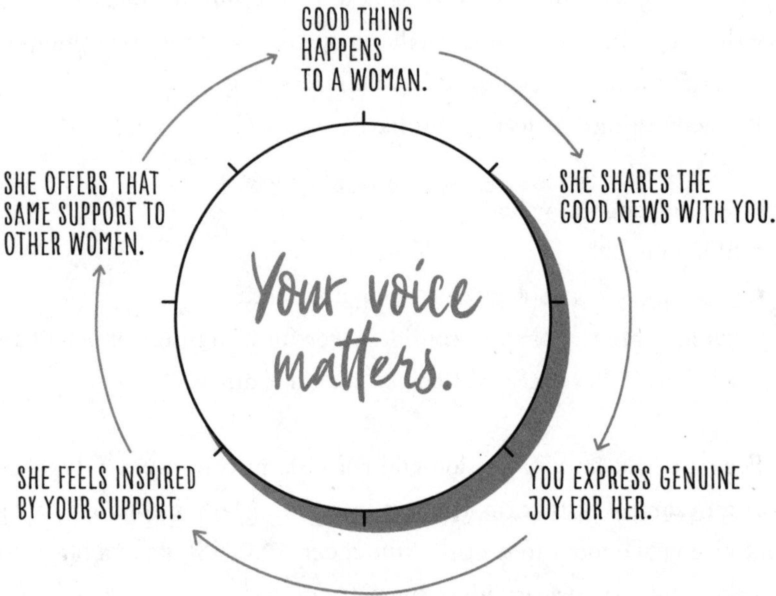

One of life's greatest joys is being able to share happy and exciting news with someone you're close to and have them celebrate for you and with you.

As I mentioned in chapter 4, when I told my fitness bestie Jen Comas I was working on a book, she replied, "I have the happiest pang of jealousy ever right now because this has always been one of my goals for myself. I'm so proud of you! You deserve this, and I can't wait to read it."

Reading her response and knowing she meant every word had me in tears. It felt good to have someone I love, and who loves me back, celebrate with me.

If you can do this for another woman, I promise you'll be giving a true gift.

Expressing Joy When You're Feeling Less Than Joyful

Are you unsure of how to feel and express joy for someone else when you're feeling jealousy, resentment, or self-pity?

Been there. And I'm happy to tell you that, like any other practice, you can get better at expressing joy.

Your best bet is to start practicing when you're not "on the spot"—that is, when you're not face-to-face with another person and expected to react joyfully in real time. Instead, practice feeling and expressing joy when someone shares good news on social media, via text message, or in an email.

The next time you hear about someone's good news and don't feel so good about it, take five to seven minutes and follow these steps:

Step #1: Notice and Name How You Feel

Yes, this again. If it's not clear by now, being aware of how you're feeling and naming it is usually the starting point for change. Plus, as you may remember, naming an emotion can help it feel less intense. Are you feeling envious? Frustrated? Depressed? Unworthy? Maybe a combination of several emotions? Once you can pinpoint how you feel, speak it out loud or write it down (e.g., "I want to be happy for Tehani and her engagement, but I'm feeling jealous and sad right now").

Step #2: Have Compassion for Yourself

These feelings are normal and they don't make you a bad person. They make you human. Once you notice and name how you feel, take a couple of deep breaths and remind yourself that this is normal. And you have the power to change it.

Step #3: Use How You Feel as a Compass

As we've discussed, we typically struggle to feel happy for someone when we are struggling ourselves, particularly in the area in which things are going well for the other person. Take a moment to dig in to why you're jealous or sad.

Is it because you want a partnership for yourself? Cool. Now that you know, you can take steps toward making yourself available for a relationship, whether emotionally, by going to therapy or doing deep self-reflection, or logistically, by signing up for a dating app or letting your friends know you're interested in being set up.

Is it because you think Tehani being engaged will take time away from your friendship? Great. Now that you've identified the issue, you can figure out ways to prioritize the friendship that work for both of you.

If you struggle to figure this out in the moment, that's okay. You can return to this step later as it's not required in order to react gracefully, but it can be a great medium- or long-term strategy to help you get introspective about what you want in and for your life.

Step #4: Spend Two Minutes Reflecting on What You're Grateful For

Gratitude is an antidote to resentment, and a powerful path toward feeling true joy.

Dr. Brené Brown, a prolific researcher and writer on shame and vulnerability (and someone whose work has changed me), said, "I have never interviewed a single person who talks about the capacity to really experience and soften into joy who does not actively practice gratitude."[2]

So when you struggle to feel happy for someone else, take two minutes to think about what you're thankful for in your own life: the roof over your head, the warm meals you have access to, your loving parents, the blue sky, your health, or even your favorite song that makes you smile every time you hear it. Imagine your body flooding with thankfulness for one or more of these things, and sit with it for two minutes.

Step #5: Envision How You'd Want Someone to React to Your Good News

Would you want them to feel resentful and self-pitying? Envious and frustrated? Or would you want them to be happy for you? Feel joy for you? Celebrate with you? Putting yourself in the other person's shoes for a moment can be a powerful way to soften your heart to their experience.

Step #6: Ask Yourself, "If I'm Being the Best Version of Myself, How Would I Reply?"

"Fake it 'til you make it" is popular advice, and I'm not saying it's wrong, but I like to ask myself this question instead. This step is less about you pretending to be a fake version of yourself and more about you invoking the best version of yourself.

The more you practice feeling happy for others when good things happen to them, the easier it gets, and the more you will feel truly happy for them.

What if you haven't had a chance to practice this skill yet, and you're hit with news you're supposed to react to on the spot? That's trickier, but my favorite tactic is the "say less" strategy. Instead of trying to figure out what to say, say little and ask questions. This prevents you from feeling like the spotlight is shining on you and your reaction.

My favorite super-short responses are:

- "Wow! That is so exciting. Tell me more."
- "Oh my gosh! How are you feeling about that?"
- "You're kidding! Congrats! Tell me everything."
- "Ah! That's huge! So what's next? What happens from here?"

These upbeat responses give the other person space to gush about their exciting news. While they're talking, focus on being present with them, and try to invoke your best self in the moment. I know you can do it.

Spotlight

» Emily Ho

Around 2009, Emily Ho started a blog called *Skinny Emmie*, with the intention of chronicling her weight loss. Over the years, her blog content changed—a lot. Instead of talking about weight loss, she started writing candidly about things like the death of her mom and her struggles with binge eating disorder, anxiety, depression, and ADHD.

"The more that I opened up and shared about these not-so-awesome things, the more love and encouragement I would get back. I would hear from other people, 'Oh, this stuff happened to me too' or 'I needed to hear this.'"

In time, Emily's blog further evolved to showcase something she loved: fashion. "I've always loved clothes, and I put some effort and investment into [finding clothes that fit me]. And so I started taking pictures of myself."

Emily said that at first, the pictures weren't anything special—"The lighting was horrendous"—but the message was well received. "People were like, 'Whoa, how do you find those clothes?'"

Emily's knowledge of how to find great clothes that fit her—knowledge she didn't think was anything special—was a huge source of interest for other women who were having trouble finding clothes in their sizes.

What's more, simply by sharing pictures of herself, Emily was helping bring visibility to an underrepresented group of women. "Typically a plus-size or fat person would be very much hidden [in media]. I want to show up for myself, but it can also inspire other people to think, 'Wait, why am I not doing that too? I can do that.'"

Over the years, Emily's blog, now called *Authentically Emmie*, moved away from weight loss and toward exploring and celebrating the needs of plus-size shoppers while representing fashion lovers of different body types.

Her work as a fashion blogger even led Emily to start her own digital media strategy business called Authentically Social.

By using her voice and authentically representing herself, Emily has expanded her ability to make an impact. She now works with a number of size-inclusive brands to help them find their authentic voice, messaging, and strategy needed to connect digitally with potential customers. This helps size-inclusive brands be more successful so they stick around longer, meaning there are more clothing options for women of all body shapes and sizes—and Emily gets to do work she loves with brands she's personally passionate about.

Emily chalks up a lot of her success to being herself. "I think that people relate to me because I've been able to show a visibly plus-size body, an unconventional—not hourglass—shape, *and* show styles from major retailers.

"People aren't coming to me just for fashion—they're coming to me because they feel like they know me. I try to share who I am, and I feel like I know a lot of them as well. At the same time, I've learned that the more I speak into discomfort, the better I feel."

Help Other Women Get Their Voices Heard

If you're a woman reading this, you've probably experienced being interrupted, spoken over, or had your ideas appropriated or ignored (often unwittingly) by your male colleagues and peers.

I say "probably" based on my experience and observations, but unfortunately, research also backs up the prevalence of this behavior.

In a 2014 study at George Washington University, researchers found that "when men were talking with women, they interrupted 33 percent more often than when they were talking with men. The men interrupted their female conversational partners 2.1 times during a three-minute conversation. That number dropped to 1.8 when they spoke to other men. The women in the study rarely interrupted their male counterparts—an average of once in a three-minute dialogue."[3]

You can counteract this situation with a strategy called "amplifying." Amplifying can help prevent women's ideas and work from being appropriated, ignored, or talked over.

A terrific story in the *Washington Post* shows amplifying in action. According to a September 2016 report, when President Barack Obama took office, two-thirds of his top aides were men. Many of those aides had worked for his campaign, which made it difficult for women new to his staff to work their way into high-up White House positions. But as more and more women entered into the important conversations, they used amplification to ensure their voices were heard.

Women on President Obama's staff began repeating one another's ideas in meetings and crediting the women who came up with them, forcing the men to acknowledge that women had just as much to contribute. One former Obama aide told the *Washington Post* that the dedication to amplifying one another's voices paid off: Obama began calling on and consulting with more women.[4]

The moral of the story? When we amplify other women, we can effect bigger change. And this strategy can be used with bosses, colleagues, peers, and social groups.

Four Ways You Can Help Women Be Fully Heard in Any Environment

STEP #1: RECOGNIZE THE PROBLEM. As you've probably learned by now, you can't fix a problem you're not aware of. The first step is to pay attention to whether this is happening in your workplace (it's less likely to happen in female-dominated workplaces) and in what settings and situations it's happening.

STEP #2: GET INTROSPECTIVE ABOUT YOUR BEHAVIOR. A 2014 informal observations study by linguist Kieran Snyder examined how frequently men and women in the tech industry interrupt one another. Her findings were as follows: men interrupted twice as much as women and were three times more likely to interrupt women as they were other men. But here's the kicker: when women *did* interrupt their colleagues, they were also *three times more likely to interrupt other women than to interrupt men*. So basically, regardless of the interrupter's gender, women are being spoken over—a lot.[5] You have an opportunity to check in with your own behavior and see where you may be contributing to the issue.

STEP #3: HAVE HONEST CONVERSATIONS WITH COLLEAGUES YOU THINK WILL BE SUPPORTIVE. Once you have more awareness of the scope of the problem in your workplace and how you contribute to it, chat with a handful of colleagues you think will support the amplification efforts. I recommend starting with other women in your office. Explain what you're learning and make a pact to join forces to amplify one another. Communicate that this strategy isn't about undiscerningly supporting one another's ideas and initiatives. Rather, it's about ensuring that women's ideas get equal airtime and consideration and that women get credit when it's due.

If your workplace has no other women and/or you have solid relationships with folks of other genders you work with, you can include them in this strategy as well. In my experience, most folks do want the women in their workplace to succeed. They're often just unaware of disparities in treatment or experience.

STEP #4: HELP OTHER WOMEN GET HEARD. Now it's time to get to work. Pay close attention in meetings and try the following strategies.

If your female colleague gets interrupted, say:	» "I'd really like to hear what Alex was saying about that. Can you let her finish?" » "I think Jo was about to get to that before she was cut off. Let's hear what she has to say and then we can circle back to you." » "Thanks so much for piping up. I want to hear your thoughts, but I'd also like to finish hearing Camille's idea before you continue."
If her idea is quickly dismissed, say:	» "Hey, Ivonne! That's an interesting idea you had a minute ago. Can you share more about that?" » "Elizabeth, a couple of minutes ago you shared an idea that I think could be beneficial. Can you share it again to make sure everyone heard it?" » "I liked what Kimberly had to say earlier, and I think her idea deserves more consideration before we move on."
If someone else suggests the same idea your female colleague already brought up, say:	» "Yes! I loved that idea when Kelsey brought it up earlier in the meeting. I'm so glad you're on board with it too." » "Hey, Sarah! You just mentioned that same idea a few minutes ago. Do you have anything to add here?" » "Thank you for circling back to Summer's idea. She always has such out-of-the-box solutions, and I think it's going to work well for us."

Say No the Right Way

Saying no might be one of the most powerful ways you can use your voice.. Yet a lot of us struggle with saying no, including me.

Saying no can be hard. As a recovering people pleaser, one of my greatest weaknesses is feeling like I'm disappointing people. Receiving a hopeful and earnest request and having to say no, thereby dashing someone's hopes and dreams? Absolute dagger. And I know many women feel the same.

As young girls, many of us are socialized to consider other people's feelings. While being considerate of other people is good, many of us do it at the expense of our own happiness, self-care, and success.

Academia provides an example of this reality. A while back, I spoke with a male senior faculty member at a large university. He told me about a trend he'd noticed in his department: faculty are asked to participate in numerous volunteer/service activities, and most of the time, the men in the department say no. They decline because they want to focus on their teaching, researching, and publishing.

The women, however, often say yes.

The faculty member (who prefers to remain anonymous) told me the following:

> I suspect there are a couple of reasons why this happens that feed off of each other. Women are more likely to say yes to service and are more likely to be asked to do service (possibly because they are more likely to say yes).
>
> I try to warn my female colleagues about not getting overcommitted to service. I hear several typical responses when I advise against taking on lots of service responsibilities:
>
> - I want to help.
> - I don't want to seem selfish.
> - I am afraid it will hurt my career if I decline.
> - Someone has to do it.
>
> These attitudes hurt female faculty because I don't think male faculty

> members hold those same attitudes—at least not as strongly. I know that I don't. I am very protective of my research time—which service, at least internal service, cuts into. This sounds selfish because it is, but I try not to be the first to volunteer for service because I know if I wait someone else will do it.

While the female faculty members might think service is necessary for their career advancement, it might be getting in the way.

A 2017 study published in *Research in Higher Education* noted that service efforts "likely have an impact on productivity in other areas of faculty effort such as research and teaching, and these latter activities can lead directly to salary differentials and overall success in academia."[6]

In other words, women are saying yes to extra service requests to the detriment of their careers.

Learning to Say No Is Important

Byron Katie said, "A dishonest yes is a no to yourself."[7] I love this powerful reminder that when we say yes to something we don't want to do or don't have time for, we must say no to something else. Saying no to things you don't want to do sets important boundaries around your time and energy, allowing you to reserve these for things you want to do.

Saying no can even be a gift to other women. When you only say yes to things you absolutely want to do, other people know that your yes isn't given begrudgingly.

Saying no also presents a chance for you to recommend another woman for the opportunity, which is a perfect example of caring for yourself and lifting other women up at the same time. Whenever possible, ask the person you'd like to recommend if they want to be recommended. Otherwise, you run the risk of putting them in a position to have to say no and wasting everyone's valuable time.

Additionally, saying no models what it looks like to set firm boundaries and care for yourself and shows women that it's not only okay but necessary for them to do the same.

Depending on how you choose to say no, you may be giving the other person a template for how they can say no in a respectful way—exactly like Dr. Krista Scott-Dixon did for me.

Krista Scott-Dixon is a legend in the health, nutrition, and behavior-change industry, having started a blog about strength training for women in 1996—eight years before I became interested in fitness and fifteen years before GGS started.

In 2013, a mutual friend of ours connected us via email and I asked Krista if she was interested in writing for GGS. Looking back, it was audacious to email someone of her caliber and ask her to write for free for my newish website, but you never know if you don't try. And I'm thankful for the naivete it took to send that email because her response was life changing for me. It showed me how to say no in a way that leaves other people feeling respected and uplifted:

> Hi Molly,
>
> Thank you so much for your generous invitation. I'm honored to be included.
>
> Right now, I'll (sadly) have to decline.
>
> I'm working on saying yes to focusing my time, resources, and energy on only a small handful of things, which means saying no to wonderful and valuable projects like these.
>
> Since I started *Stumptuous* in the mid-1990s as a deliberately noncommercial resource, money for me is obviously less important than putting good stuff out into the world and being part of a community of people trying to make positive change. I'm guessing you share this perspective to some degree.
>
> So for me, it's really only an issue of limited capacity. (Which I'm recently coming to terms with. Apparently I am not a superhero who lives in a universe of thirty-hour days and infinite energy.)
>
> I think your project is super, and I've long been a fan. I hope you have great success with it.
>
> Please drop me a line in six months or so; my situation and life demands might be different, and I might be more able to help you out.
>
> All the best,
>
> Krista (KSD)

As with any skill, you can learn to say no. You can begin with the following tips:

Tip #1: Start Small

You've already learned that the best way to kick off any new practice is to start small and build your confidence and momentum from there. Start by saying "no thank you" to an offer to refill your water at a restaurant or turning down a second helping of dinner at your mom's house. Getting comfortable saying no in these lower-stakes situations will allow you to practice this skill without much risk.

Tip #2: Expect That You'll Disappoint People

A huge reason many women struggle to say no is that we hate disappointing people, and we want to be liked and seen as agreeable. So if you're worried you'll disappoint people . . . well, you will. The bad news is that this sucks. The good news is that you know it will happen, and being aware removes the fear of the unknown. If you anticipate that you'll disappoint people, you can put measures in place to soften the blow if you like.

Tip #3: Trust That Relationships That Matter Can Handle Disappointment

People who love you want you to be happy, and that typically means they want you to make decisions that are good for you. If you have a close relationship with someone and they take your nos personally or get offended when you set boundaries, that is their issue to work on—you're not responsible for that. You can let them know you care about them and don't like disappointing them, but you must stay firm with your boundaries to be respectful of yourself.

Tip #4: Remember That No Is a Complete Sentence (But Context Can Help)

While I deeply believe "No" and "No, thank you" are complete sentences and women don't have to explain their nos, if you have the desire and capacity to provide context for your no, it's possible to do so in an honest, straightforward way that leaves the other person feeling good and uplifted. Krista's no was a great example of that.

Tip #5: Reward Yourself for Saying No

Set up some kind of small reward system for yourself each time you say no. External rewards can be a powerful incentive to change human behavior, so rewarding yourself each time you say no might be the extra motivation you need to do it. It could be as simple as putting one dollar in a jar every time you say no, to save up for something you want. Or you could keep a note on your phone, tracking each thing you say no to and how long it would have taken you to do the requested action. At the end of the week, see how much time you've "banked" by saying no, and use that time to treat yourself to something you want to do, like a long walk listening to your favorite podcast, an afternoon nap, or undistracted time with your kids where you're super present.

Learn to Recover from Saying the Wrong Thing

Sometimes the wrong thing spills out of our mouths before we even think about it.

I just finished sharing all these great strategies for saying no, right? But sometimes I have not only failed to follow this advice but also found myself accidentally offering help when I didn't have capacity to do so.

Case in point: a while ago I was chatting with my friend Dr. Brooke Kalanick (the same Brooke who was part of the ripple effect that led to the creation of this book). At the end of our conversation, I text-blurted, "Beyond what we've chatted about, is there anything else I can do to help?"

My immediate thought was, *Shit. Why did I do that?* I was drowning in work and truly incapable of doing more. And yet I instinctively asked what else I could help with. (Facepalm!)

It was so automatic, it flew out of my fingers before I even realized what I'd done.

She enthusiastically accepted and replied with some other ways I could help.

I felt momentarily trapped.

I care deeply about my friend and wanted to help, but I knew I couldn't. So I took a deep breath and wrote her a brutally honest reply.

I explained what happened and told her I didn't have the capacity to do anything else right now. I also told her I was in a shame spiral and was sweating and was going to go hide in my closet.

This might not seem like a big deal to some folks, but for a people pleaser in recovery like me, this is huge because disappointing people has always been hard for me. Ten minutes later—which feels like an eternity when you're sweating and hiding in your closet—Brooke texted me back, and of course, it was fine. She was gracious and told me not to worry about it.

In that moment, I not only prioritized my needs but I *relearned* four important lessons (because what is life if we aren't relearning lessons we already know?):

1. My needs are important and deserve to be prioritized.
2. Honesty is *always* best, and saying how you're feeling in the moment is helpful.
3. True friendships can handle hard, awkward, uncomfortable conversations.
4. People who love you will respect your needs and boundaries.

Most of all, if you say the wrong thing, you can always go back and correct yourself. (You'll learn more about how to recover from mistakes in chapter 10.)

Next Steps

In this chapter I shared several ways you can use your voice to lift other women up. Below you'll find exercises to guide you through each of the main topics of this chapter, including how to:

» Share your story
» Respond to criticism
» Share your good news
» Celebrate other women's good news
» Help other women get their voices heard
» Say no the right way
» Recover from saying the wrong thing

Most of these exercises will need to be done in the future, as the opportunities arise and as you continue to read this book—although a few can be done right away. You can get started immediately if you want, or return to these exercises once you've finished the book or whenever it's right for you.

To download your resource guide, visit:
www.MollyGalbraith.com/book-resources

Exercise #1: Share Your Story

1. Now that you understand the power of sharing your story with other women, I encourage you to start thinking about what story you might want to share.* For example:

---

* If you don't know what story you want to share yet, that's okay. Chapter 9 will give you a lot of clarity about how you might want to help other women.

- Is there something you've wanted to share with a friend or a family member for a while, but haven't?
- Have you been through loss or struggle you think will help other women feel less alone?
- Have you accomplished something you think will inspire other women?

Jot down some ideas, and the details of how you want to share and with whom. Would you feel more comfortable in a one-on-one setting with a close friend? Sharing over dinner with a few of your family members? Or sharing on social media or in a blog? Write down some thoughts below.

2. Once you share your story with someone, record the details:

- What story did you share?
- With whom did you share it?
- How did you share it, and in what context?
- How was it received?

Exercise #2: Respond to Criticism

Now that you have a better idea of what story you might want to share and through which medium, reflect on how you might respond to criticism.

1. If you've already shared your story with someone, did they respond with criticism? If not, how might other folks respond to your story with criticism? What might they do or say? What negative ways might they react? Writing down these possibilities allows you to better handle and respond (or not respond) to this criticism when it arises.

2. Consider what you want your response to criticism to be. Remember the four-step process you learned about:

» Respond instead of react.
» Check in with your energy.
» Check in with your values.
» Give people the benefit of the doubt.

Of course, this isn't the only way to handle criticism. Some people take all criticism as feedback and consider criticism deeply. Some people brush it off completely. Take time to consider how *you* want to respond.

Exercise #3: Share Your Good News

Now that you know about the positive ripple effect you can create by sharing your good news, it's time to brainstorm what you might share and with whom.

Like any other new habit or behavior, starting small and simple can help you feel more comfortable putting this into practice. Write down a couple of examples of people with whom you might share your good news and what you might share with them.

Exercise #4: Celebrate Other Women's Good News

Time to celebrate other women and their good news! The next time you hear about someone's good news and aren't feeling happy about it, take five to seven minutes and go through these six steps, jotting down answers where necessary:

1. Notice and name how you feel.
2. Have compassion for yourself.
3. Use how you feel as a compass—why are you feeling how you're feeling?
4. Spend two minutes writing down what you're grateful for in your own life.
5. Envision how you'd want someone to react to your good news.
6. Ask yourself, *If I'm being the best version of myself, how would I reply?*

Exercise #5: Help Other Women Get Their Voices Heard

1. To ensure your coworkers are heard and their ideas are fairly considered, answer the following questions:

- Is this an issue in my workplace? How can I know for certain? Have I heard others complain about this issue?

- Is this something I've done to others? How might I be contributing to the problem? How can I do better?

- Who else might be open to recognizing this problem? How can I explain this to them and gain their support?

2. Practice what you might say when your female colleague isn't heard. The more you practice, the more prepared you'll be when the time comes to speak up.

   Imagine the following situations happen to a woman you work with. What would you say if . . .

- . . . your colleague gets interrupted?

- . . . her idea was quickly dismissed?

- . . . someone suggested the same idea she already had and tried to take credit for it?

Exercise #6: Say No the Right Way

Saying no can be a powerful way to use your voice, preserve your precious time and energy, and model boundaries for other women. It can also be a powerful way to recommend other women and expand their access to opportunities.

Earlier in this chapter I gave you tips for learning how to say no. Not all of them require engaging in a specific exercise, but starting small and setting up a reward system for saying no can prepare you for the nos you're about to say:

1. What are some small ways you can practice saying no in your life right away?

2. What type of reward system could you set up to encourage yourself to say no more often?

3. Time to practice! Imagine you're invited to partake in a special service project organized by your boss or close friend. You'd love to participate, but you're unable to due to time constraints. Write an email to the person, telling them you can't do it. (There's a template provided in the Companion Resource Guide if you need more help).

4. Now consider applying this in your own life.

- What are some activities you'd like to say no to that you've found yourself saying yes to?
- What would it look like to say no? You can use the template in the Companion Resource Guide, if it's helpful for you.
- What might someone say in return if you said no?
- How could you handle that?

Exercise #7: Recover from Saying the Wrong Thing

Sometimes when we're interacting with others, we make mistakes and say the wrong thing.

1. Using the guidance I provided earlier in the chapter, write down a scenario in which you said the wrong thing and either need to apologize or otherwise make a situation right.

2. Now flip the script and write down a scenario in which you said nothing, and how you might revisit that situation and say what you wish you had said.

CHAPTER 9

Using Your Superpowers for Good

There are so many different ways to be brilliant. I believe that you and every human being is born with masterful gifts.

—**BEYONCÉ**

CHAPTER 9

Using Your Superpowers for Good

We all have a finite amount of time on the planet. It's important that we live true to ourselves, look for small ways we can lift women up each day—and make the most of our own unique superpowers.

I think of superpowers as a combination of our values, our knowledge/skills/talents, our passion, and our resources. Our superpowers are kind of like our values, but turbocharged.

You've already learned about finding your values, using your voice, and making small efforts each day in a way that creates a powerful ripple effect. Using your superpowers builds on all that; it means tapping in even more deeply to what sets you on fire, what excites you, what you're great at, and what you're capable of doing to make your best contribution to the world.

Before finding my superpowers, I often felt unsure how to spend my time, energy, and resources. It felt like I was on a road trip with no map and no idea of my final destination. My values might have helped me see who I was and what I stand for . . . but where was I going? Finding my superpowers gave me direction. It was like getting access to a roadmap designed just for me that uncovered *my* unique path to lifting women up.

The same can be true of you. In this chapter, I'll give you ideas about how you might be able to put your superpowers into action. What you'll read here is by no means a complete list of the important gifts you may have to share with the world or all the amazing things you can do to lift women up. Rather, these ideas represent some of the ways I've seen women make a big impact. Think of this chapter as an "inspiration menu": a starting point to help you imagine how you might lift women up by using the resources, skills, talents, and/or passion that you have.

At the end of this chapter I'll walk you through exactly how to find your superpowers, step-by-step. If you'd like, you can jump ahead to the end of this chapter and do the "Next Steps" section first. Or you can read on, gather inspiration, and then use the exercises in that section to figure out how to put this into action in your own life, whenever you're ready.

How I Tapped into My Superpowers

As you know, in my late twenties I realized that I wanted to help lift women up.

But how? What was the best way for me to do that?

By that point I was already running Girls Gone Strong, but I still didn't have clarity about the exact ways I could make the most difference or have the biggest impact.

In order to clarify my path forward, I needed to take stock of my superpowers. So, I considered my values, skills, knowledge and talents, passion, and resources—just as you'll learn how to do at the end of this chapter.

Here's what that looked like:

MOLLY'S SUPERPOWERS

Top Value	» making a difference
Skills, Knowledge, and Talents	» seventeen years of coaching experience, and as a generalist, I have a very broad base of health, fitness, nutrition, body image, pre- and postnatal, and change psychology knowledge » the ability to speak and write in a way that most can *hear* my message, even if they disagree » being able to see and honor multiple perspectives » taking complex and seemingly opposing topics and breaking them down in easy-to-understand ways » emotional resilience and unwavering optimism

	» connecting with other women » envisioning, reimagining, and creating new ideas and solutions » an understanding of how to make education transformative
Driving Passion	» to help women and health and fitness professionals who work with women
Resources/ Assets	» time » platform » network (I have access to a network of world-class health and fitness experts from different disciplines across the globe.)
Superpower Statement	I use my knowledge, skills, time, network, and platform to create evidence-based, interdisciplinary, women-specific health, fitness, and nutrition education for women and health and fitness professionals to make a difference for women and the industry as a whole.

When I was able to recognize and combine my knowledge, skills, values, passions, and resources, suddenly, my superpowers—and sense of purpose and direction—were far clearer. That's when I realized GGS could make the biggest difference creating educational programs and certifications for women and health and fitness professionals who work with women.

Boom.

I had it: my roadmap, my guide to spending my time, clarity about what to say yes to and what to say no to. And a strong sense of passion and purpose about how I could use my own unique gifts, abilities, and resources to help lift women up.

My partner, Casey, and I knew that creating these educational programs and certifications would increase the number of health and fitness professionals worldwide who have the knowledge and skills required to confidently coach women.

If you're not in the health and fitness industry, you may not know there's very little education that speaks specifically to women's unique and varied anatomy, physiology, and lived experiences. That gives comprehensive, evidence-based information about pelvic health, hormonal issues, body image struggles, menstrual cycles, and menopause. And this lack of information is keeping women from getting the coaching they deserve.

So we created two comprehensive coaching certifications: our GGS Women's Coaching Specialist Certification covers coaching adult women across their lifespan, and our GGS Pre- & Postnatal Coaching Certification covers coaching women specifically during pregnancy and postpartum.

I'm incredibly passionate about this work because when women feel strong, confident, and empowered in their lives and bodies, we can change the world.* It's especially exciting to me because I could see the potential for a huge ripple effect. Every coach or trainer we help is working with 10–150+ clients, and that amplifies the difference we can make significantly, both in those women's lives and in our industry as a whole.

What's more, the women who take our certifications now get to do meaningful work they love, while lifting women up, and starting a ripple effect of their own.

While those were my superpowers, I had obstacles to overcome as well. (As everyone does.) A big one was limited access to financial resources. To deal with this, Casey and I spent years bootstrapping the organization. Every time we created a program, we took all the profits from that program and reinvested them back into the organization. While it wasn't easy, we felt like more opportunity needed to be created for women and there was potential for GGS to do something about it.

I won't lie: doing this work has involved a lot of effort and sacrifice, but because I do it by harnessing my superpowers, it feels incredibly fulfilling and joyful. I'm able to tap into what I'm best at, what I really care about, and that

* That's actually our mission statement at GGS: We create evidence-based, interdisciplinary health, fitness, and nutrition resources for women and professionals who work with women. Because when women feel strong, confident, and empowered in their lives and bodies, we can change the world.

fuels me. It allows me to work passionately without burning myself out so I can sustain my work over the long haul.

This is the magic of finding your superpowers and using them in service of the difference you want to make.

Our Time Here Is Limited. Why Waste It on Something That Isn't Really *You*?

There are so many ways to lift women up, and the best way to make an impact is by drawing upon the things that are unique to us: the things we love, the things that light us up, the things we have in spades.

Here's a quick look at how this translates in my life.

I use my superpowers to:

- work with a diverse group of leading health professionals from many disciplines to create educational materials (like the certifications mentioned above and *tons* of content that's completely free for our community like articles, courses, and downloadable materials)
- reinvest a portion of the revenue generated from our certifications back into full and partial scholarships to our coaching certifications, with a strong emphasis on Black women, Women of Color, and women of fewer socioeconomic means within our global community
- donate to organizations, causes, and individuals that align with my values (more on this below)
- act in other small ways daily, like buying from women-owned businesses, sharing other women's work, sharing my own story, giving credit where it's due, amplifying other women's voices, and more. I can take these actions because they align with my values and don't take much time, which is now my scarcest resource.

To do those things, there's plenty that I say no to. My time doesn't allow me to mentor or volunteer much. I've turned down major deals and partnership opportunities in order to stay focused. And I almost never engage in online "fights" or social media "pile-ons" because I find them to be ineffective (as opposed to calling in and one-on-one conversations, which are far more effective for me), and they can eat up a lot time—time that I need to serve our business, team, and community.

We all have superpowers, but that doesn't mean we're superhuman. It's important that we choose wisely about how we spend our time. (And if you ever have trouble saying no, just refer back to chapter 8 on how to do exactly that.)

Using Your Superpowers: Your Inspiration Menu

How will *you* use your superpowers to make a difference? Here are some ways you can make a difference depending on your own unique blend of values, skills/knowledge/talents, passion, and resources.

Remember, this is by no means a comprehensive list. Rather, I've chosen these as options to (hopefully) inspire you because I've been inspired by the women I know using these tactics to make a difference for women and girls. Take a look, and see what gets you excited!

Mentoring, Teaching, and Sharing Insider Knowledge

The biggest inspiration for this superpower comes from my maternal grandmother, Helen, who I called Gama.

Gama prepped kids for the ACT and SAT and tutored high-level math for many years. At eighty-eight years old she had a stroke, but even afterward, she still tutored.

One day, when she was ninety, I asked her a math question, something to the effect of, "Apples cost sixty cents. Johnny buys three apples. He has five dollars. How much money does he have left over?"

Gama grinned and asked, "With or without sales tax?"

That was typical of her. I walked into her room about six months before she died, and she looked up at me and placed a book on her chest. It was an SAT prep guide. She was reading that book because she wanted to help her nurse's aides, who wanted to go back to school, study for their exams. Her desire to help other women get educated never faded, and you can do the same.

Helping women develop their skills or knowledge doesn't always have to be done through formal learning or education. Simply sharing stories about your own experience can be a powerful way to do this. One of my mentors I mentioned earlier is John Berardi, PhD, cofounder of the nutrition coaching company Precision Nutrition (PN). One of John's principles is that he doesn't necessarily give advice—he tells stories. In all his years of mentorship, he's almost never told me what to do with Girls Gone Strong. Instead, he tells me stories and examples of what they did at PN and how it worked or didn't work. I've found this approach really helpful, as it's not prescriptive or restrictive. When you share your experience instead of telling someone what to do, the other person can take what they want from your story.

Don't underplay your knowledge or experiences. If you have professional knowledge, it can be incredibly important to other women because you might be able to help more women get qualified and succeed in your industry or area of specialty.

Here are a few ways you can be a mentor:

- If you're a business owner and you don't have an internship or mentorship program, you can create one specifically for women/girls who want more experience in your field.
- If you work at a big facility or corporation, you can talk to your manager or boss about creating an internship/mentorship program for women/girls.
- If you're a solopreneur, consider mentoring a woman/girl for a period of time, such as two to three months of the year or while you're working on a finite project.
- If you're a graduate, check out university and college mentorship programs through your alumni association.
- Volunteer with an organization like Big Brothers Big Sisters of America and mentor a child to help her reach her full potential.
- If you have a special skill or knowledge (for example, you're a math whiz like my Gama), consider offering tutoring services within your community.

(Some of these could even fill the critical "experience gap" potential employers often tell women is holding them back from getting the job they're applying for.)

If being a mentor sounds overwhelming, never fear. You don't have to be involved in formal mentorship to pass along what you know in a helpful way. Sometimes you can lift women up simply by sharing insider knowledge.

Insider knowledge is information about a person, team, or system that someone less experienced wouldn't know offhand. It might seem counterintuitive to share this information since many of us are inclined to hoard insights like these to help ourselves advance. But that's scarcity mindset popping up again. In reality, sharing insider knowledge helps everyone do better, and the relationships you form from sharing can be a huge future benefit to you.

Here's what sharing insider knowledge can look like in practice—and why it's so important.

A few years ago I was asked to speak at a sought-after fitness industry event called Perform Better. Perform Better hosts four three-day summits every year, geared toward health and fitness professionals. Being asked to speak is a pretty big deal.

Shortly after the announcement was made that I'd be speaking at the event, a woman named Rachel Cosgrove reached out to me. Rachel was one of just a handful of women who had been on the Perform Better circuit for a long time. She has over two decades of experience in the health and fitness industry, and she and her husband, Alwyn, own Results Fitness in Santa Clarita, California. Results Fitness is often credited for pioneering the small-group coaching model and at one point was one of the highest (if not the highest) revenue-per-square-foot gym in America. Rachel also has written two books with *Women's Health* magazine and is considered one of the most successful women in fitness.

When Rachel saw my name as a presenter at the event, she could have had several different reactions.

She could have felt territorial over another woman joining the conference circuit. She could have been judgmental and made assumptions about whether or not I belonged there. She could have minded her own business and not said a word. But she didn't. The minute Rachel saw my name, she emailed me and said:

> Hey! I'm so happy to see your name on the list for Perform Better this year.
>
> I'd love to hop on a call with you and give you the scoop on how the Perform Better summits work so you can be as successful as possible and stay on the circuit for a really long time.

What followed was amazing. Not only was it an informative phone conversation with one of my fitness coaching idols, but I got to experience the magic that happens when a strong woman lifts another woman up.

Rather than keep that valuable information to herself, Rachel chose to share it.

That made a huge difference to me. And it's a great reminder that information and insider knowledge can be extremely useful for helping women achieve and maintain a higher level of success.

Here are some more examples of what that "insider knowledge" might look like. Imagine a new female colleague arrives on the scene:

Examples of Insider Knowledge About a Person	What does this person need to know about certain coworkers? What's the best way to communicate with different team members? Is there something your boss likes done in a particular way?
Examples of Insider Knowledge About a Workplace	What are some of the unwritten rules of this workplace? What do you wish you'd known when you first started? Has anyone ever made a major mistake that could be useful to know about?
Examples of Insider Knowledge About an Industry	Who are the important players in this industry? Who should a newcomer follow/meet/get to know? (Bonus points if you can make the intro!) What are some of the best places to meet people and/or get information (e.g., events, newsletters, forums, social channels, conferences, etc.)? What books or courses should she read or take?

Hiring and Referring Women

Girls Gone Strong has always been a women-led* organization, and it's important to us that our employees, contractors, and collaborators represent a diverse range of qualified women, but we certainly have room to grow and do better. I'm no expert in this area, so I brought in my dear friend, GGS consultant and HR expert, Colene Elridge, to share important tips on how you can hire women and support the creation of diverse teams within your organization, which you'll find below. (Fun fact: our team worked with Colene to develop our mission, vision, values, and hiring policies and practices for GGS!)

Before we dive into how to do it, let's talk about why it's important.

If you're in a position to hire women and increase the diversity on your team, you can intentionally create a ripple effect that leads to huge, important change. You're providing more opportunities for women, and those women may go on to inspire, mentor, role model, and even hire other women in your industry.

And building a diverse business isn't just a "feel good" decision—it's also a business decision. Evidence shows that diverse teams—that is, teams that have a diverse range of different backgrounds, genders, ages, geographic locations, and races—make more money. They're more profitable and they make better decisions faster than homogeneous teams.[1]

That said, choices related to hiring inevitably raise questions, such as: How do you hire more women while ensuring you choose the best person for the job? How do you create a more diverse and inclusive environment and support women within your organization, without tokenizing or alienating some people? That's precisely what Colene is here to teach us.

---

* Yes, we do have some men on our team, including my life and business partner, Casey. Though he operates mostly behind the scenes, he's an integral part of running the day-to-day business at Girls Gone Strong, and we'd definitely not have had the impact and success we've had without his help.

Tips for Hiring Women and Creating Diverse Teams

From Colene Elridge (aka the coolest person you haven't met), a coach and consultant who's passionate about helping women transform the way they lead and live.

Tip #1: Do an Audit of Your Current Hiring Process

It's important to look at how your process typically works and understand where you have room for improvement.

For example, you might consider the number of applications you typically receive for a job posting. Given those applications, what percentage are "diverse" applicants, and where do they drop off along the way?

From there you might consider: Where is the leak, and where are the gaps in that process? Is it in the initial intake where you're not getting enough diverse applicants applying for the jobs? Or is it in the screening process? Are those unconscious biases getting in the way of how your team is viewing the applications? Or is it in the interview process?

At the same time, you might consider looking for the strengths and weaknesses in your process because I do think it's important to say, "What do we do really well? And how do we capitalize on that?"

That way, you can work on fixing your weaknesses while also capitalizing on your strengths.

Tip #2: Set Specific Goals

Let's say you want to diversify your sales team. You might say, "Okay, our goal is to have 15 percent visible diversity on the sales team within the next year." That's a measurable goal, allowing you to see how much progress you have (or haven't) made.

I recommend choosing one metric to improve at a time. A lot of organizations try to do all of the things at the same time, and then they do none of it well.

Picking one metric may be a slower process, but you usually end up with a larger gain and a lot more commitment along the way.

Tip #3: Consider How and Where You're Sourcing Applicants

Where are you looking for candidates? Let's be honest: if you're just going over to your friend Bob's house and asking him if he has a recommendation, of course you're not going to have a diverse applicant pool.

You might explore posting your position in a wide array of publications or spaces—anything that's going to broaden the scope of the reach you can have. That way, you're not utilizing the same sources over and over again.

One way to source from a more diverse pool is to encourage referrals from your current employees. In fact, incentivizing employees for diverse candidate referrals is a great way to increase your intake of diverse applications. Some people think that's weird because why would I ask my employees to send me a list of diverse candidates? But it's no different than saying, "We really value diversity. If you work here, that means you know what the company culture is, and we value your input. Here's what we're looking for . . ."

Another option is to use a recruiting firm. A lot of outsourcing companies have tools that can help eliminate subconscious bias by removing details like the person's name, address, and graduation year (i.e., the kinds of things that might create accidental bias) and simply reviewing the facts.

Tip #4: Demonstrate Your Appreciation for Diversity

Are inclusivity and diversity important to your organization? Then include them in your stated values!

Beyond that, make it clear: What does diversity mean to your organization? Why is it important to you? State this on your website.

Further, how are you demonstrating that diversity is important—not just for new candidates or employees but for existing employees, customers, and everyone you work with?

Are you celebrating your organization's current diversity? Are there employee resource groups? Are you using diverse suppliers? Where are you spending your money? How are you showing both your internal employees and external candidates how much you value diversity?

Demonstrate your appreciation of diversity throughout your organizational culture, not just when trying to attract diverse candidates. For example, are you participating in Pride? Are you celebrating Hispanic heritage month? Or Juneteenth?

If not, start now! If you wait until you get a Hispanic employee and then suddenly start celebrating Hispanic heritage month, that can feel uncomfortable, shine the spotlight on the Hispanic employee, and feel tokenizing and isolating for them. Instead, make celebrating these a part of your culture now.

Tip #5: Foster an Inclusive Company Culture

In addition to demonstrating your appreciation for diversity, what are you doing within your company, with your current employees, to create an inclusive culture?

I define *inclusion* as a state of feeling valued, respected, and supported. So how are you valuing your employees? How are you respecting your employees? How are you supporting your employees?

Create a clear company culture that says: This is what we stand for, and we stand for inclusion. Regardless of who you are, we will value you because of the work you do. Regardless of who you are, we will respect you, and we will support you because you're a member of our team.

Tip #6: Start with Management

Oftentimes, I see companies try to hire diverse candidates at the bottom level because typically those jobs don't require as many skills or as much education. So they'll utilize the lower-level positions as a means to diversify their organization. The problem with that is you have so many things you'll be unaware of if you don't have that representation throughout the entire organization.

On the other hand, bringing diversity into the management level shows the validity of having a diverse team and why it's important. It also shows that a company puts their money where their mouth is.

Of course, you must be intentional about this pursuit because, at the management level, positions are competitive for diverse candidates. Plus, if you're just bringing in someone to be the Person of Color or the woman on the executive team, and you're not showing that person that you value, respect, and support them, they'll leave, and that won't benefit them or your organization. That said, if you do it right, starting with the management level before bringing in other employees, you will receive the greatest long-term gains and benefits.

If you're not in a position to hire women, no problem. Refer or recommend them!

If I love someone's services, I'll talk about them nonstop because it's fun and easy for me to rave about a woman who I think is doing great work.

If you know of someone who's hiring, think about the women you know. Is there anyone you could recommend?

Referring women has many benefits, including helping them break into male-dominated industries or teams. Even if a job isn't a match, you're helping them create deeper relationships and grow their opportunities. Plus, when a woman finds out you referred her, that boosts her confidence. After all, you're willing to put your name on the line!

Whether you're hiring or referring, ensure that you're paying the women you hire equitably. For years, doing pay equity analysis was an incredibly time-consuming and expensive process. Today, software can quickly find pay issues based on gender, race, or any other category, help you fix those issues, help you stay in compliance over time, and even help you calculate safe ranges for new hires in order to maintain overall pay equity.*

Creating Something New

You've no doubt heard the expression "Necessity is the mother of invention"—that is, the driving force for creating something new is filling a need.

If you've ever thought to yourself:

- *I wish someone had created ____.*
- *Wouldn't it be nice if _____ existed?*
- *Why hasn't someone come up with _____ already?*

Maybe that "someone" is you!

A "creation" can be anything, including but not limited to:

- coaching services
- an informational product
- a physical product
- a nonprofit organization, fundraiser, or drive

---

* One option is Syndio, a software-as-a-service (SaaS) operation headed up by Chief Executive Officer Maria Colacurcio. Soon after their inception, Maria and her team at Syndio were hired by major organizations like Match Group and Slack.

- new software or technology
- an in-person event
- a digital platform or space

And it can range from a full-blown entrepreneurial venture to a side hustle to a small creative project or hobby.

Creating something new could mean starting your own:

- coaching business that focuses on women
- community (think about Jennifer Lau, whom you read about in chapter 4, or Jameela Jamil and Sonja R. Price Herbert, whom you read about in chapter 5)
- event (like Allison Tenney, whom you also read about in chapter 5)
- nonprofit organization (which you'll read about below)
- movement (like Girls Gone Strong)

Or, you can create a fundraiser. In November 2018, that's what one writer, lecturer, public academic—and someone I deeply admire and appreciate—did. Her name is Rachel Cargle.

Rachel knew that major barriers affect access to mental health treatment for Black women and girls, such as:

- expense (therapy typically ranges from $80 to $200 per session)
- transportation to and from therapy, which, depending on where someone lives, can cost money and take lots of time
- difficulty finding a licensed mental health professional who is also Black and deeply understands their situation and life experiences
- trauma of sharing all of their pain on a written application to be reviewed by others and then determined "worthy" of therapy and/or financial assistance

Rachel wanted to help. So, she decided to host a birthday fundraiser called Therapy for Black Women and Girls.

Rachel has a big following on social media, so her fundraiser in late 2018 went a long way—raising more than $250,000, which made it possible for Black women and girls across the United States to receive therapy support and healing that will impact future generations.

She then created the Loveland Foundation, the official continuation of her original effort to bring opportunity and healing to communities of color and especially to Black women and girls. Through their partnerships with Therapy for Black Girls, National Queer and Trans Therapists of Color Network, Talkspace, and Open Path Collective, Loveland Foundation Therapy Fund recipients "have access to a comprehensive list of mental health professionals across the country providing high quality, culturally competent services to Black women and girls."[2]

These partnerships also increase the likelihood that participants can financially afford therapy after the four to eight sessions supported by the Loveland Foundation Therapy Fund.*

These examples are powerful, but let's not forget: you can start small. And you don't have to have a huge social media following or raise $250,000 like Rachel in order to make an impact. In fact, when I first connected with Rachel on Instagram in March 2018, she was raising money to cover the cost of admission for young Black girls to see the Disney version of *A Wrinkle in Time* so they could go to a movie where someone who looked like them was the main character. Her small fundraiser allowed dozens of Black girls the opportunity to enjoy an afternoon of fun, entertainment, and seeing themselves as the hero of the story.

If you want to raise money for a cause, you can organize a walkathon, a car wash, or a neighborhood yard sale. Or you can do a drive for things like:

- clothing for women (and their children) who are escaping intimate partner violence

* In 2020, the Loveland Foundation Therapy Fund is projected to cover over 8,000 hours of free therapy support for Black women and girls nationwide. In addition to the therapy fund, the Loveland Foundation hopes to contribute to the empowerment and liberation of the communities they serve through fellowships, residency programs, listening tours, and more. Learn more at https://thelovelandfoundation.org/about/.

- food for kids who struggle with food insecurity on the weekends when they're not in school
- school supplies for children in low-income neighborhoods whose schools aren't well-equipped
- menstrual products for women who cannot afford them, particularly those who are experiencing housing insecurity and have to choose between food and menstrual products
- household items for refugees who have recently relocated to your area

Have less time and energy? A fundraiser can be as simple as a giving circle you organize, where you and eleven of your friends and family members each donate twenty dollars a month. Each month one of you picks the charity or cause it goes to support, or you vote on a new cause to donate to.

Or during the holidays, in lieu of gifts, you can donate money to a fundraising pool and use that money to buy gifts and supplies for people in need or donate to a local charity. That's what my family does each Christmas. We have a large family, and instead of a massive gift exchange, we each draw a name out of a hat and buy one gift, then donate money to a fund that goes to support families struggling to provide for themselves and their children. Of course, make sure you pair up with those whose values align with yours to ensure you feel good about your donation.

Volunteering

If time is a resource you currently have to donate, or you're passionate about service and want to find the time to donate, volunteering can be a powerful way to lift other women up. Quickly googling "volunteer opportunities near me" or visiting a site like volunteermatch.org can show you a plethora of options to explore.

Here are just a handful of the endless possibilities:

- Transportation volunteer
- Crisis counselor
- Girl Scout troop leader
- English as a second language (ESL) tutor

- Youth mentor
- Life skills mentor for folks reentering society after incarceration
- Refugee resettlement volunteer
- Food bank volunteer

If you don't have a lot of extra hours each week, you can get creative. One example I've seen is women creating a childcare co-op with two or three other women. They take turns watching one another's kids one day a week or swap doing the sports practice pickups and drop-offs one day each week. In doing so, they pool their resources, help one another out, and free up a significant amount of time in their own schedule on days when the other women are watching the kids or doing the pickups and drop-offs.

I've also seen something similar with a meal exchange. A group of women get together, and they each do a huge batch cook. They then exchange meals, so each person cooks once that week and they have several different home-cooked meals to serve their families throughout the week.

One thing to keep in mind is what I mentioned in the previous chapter about how we as women can feel obligated to volunteer our time. Remember, you don't owe anyone your time. (Okay, okay—this is a reminder to me as well!)

Donating and Investing

While I grew up without financial stability for most of my childhood, I also grew up watching my parents aim to make a difference with what they had.

One day, my dad came home from work wearing nothing but a T-shirt, and he had a towel wrapped around his waist. When my mom asked him where his pants were, he said he gave them to a hitchhiker he picked up who seemed down on his luck. They were my dad's only pair of pants.

Of course, you don't have to donate to charity (or give away your last pair of pants!) to make a difference. And I'm definitely not suggesting that you give away money you don't have. But if you have the financial means to donate or invest in women, it can be an impactful way to support women, and every little bit helps. I started donating very small amounts of money over a decade ago and have increased my donations as my access to financial resources has increased.

Donating money is a very personal decision, so I encourage you to tap into your highest values and what issues deeply matter to you. I'll walk you through my approach, but don't feel pressured to follow my system if it isn't the right fit for you.

STEP #1: I start with a monthly budget that I feel comfortable donating. I have a handful of charities I give to regularly on a monthly auto debit, and I leave space in my budget for more spontaneous donations that I want to make when timely situations arise.

STEP #2: Throughout the month, I donate to different timely causes as I learn about them—like helping people struggling after a natural disaster or a woman in the GGS community who's fundraising for her child's surgery.

STEP #3: At the end of the year, I look at our budget and see what might be left to donate, to ensure we've given what we wanted without putting ourselves in a difficult position financially.

I try to give to a wide variety of charities that align with my values and that I think are doing good in the world. Some examples include:

My Value	Organizations I Feel Represent That Value
WOMEN'S HEALTH AND BODY AUTONOMY	I donate to Planned Parenthood. I was able to get a pelvic exam and birth control there totally free of cost many years ago and feel passionate about helping women get access to reproductive health care and education, including birth control, condoms, pre- and postnatal exams, and other tests and exams that help women stay healthy and allow them to have more control over planning if and when to have children.

ANTIRACISM AND PRO-LIBERATION FOR BLACK, INDIGENOUS, AND PEOPLE OF COLOR (BIPOC)	I give to different charities that support folks in marginalized communities, like Rachel Cargle's Loveland Foundation, which pairs Black licensed mental health professionals with Black women and girls who need mental health services, Black Mamas Matter, an organization to advance Black maternal health, or the International Rescue Committee, whose mission is to help people whose lives and livelihoods have been shattered by conflict and disaster to survive, recover, and gain control of their futures.
HUMANITARIANISM	I've been directly sponsoring a young boy in South America through ChildFund for more than ten years, and I often donate to Together Rising, an organization started by Glennon Doyle that "transforms collective heartbreak into effective action."[4] They work directly with leaders in the communities they're helping to determine how funds are best spent.
RESILIENCE AND SELF-SUFFICIENCY	I also often give Christmas gifts to Heifer International, a "global nonprofit working to eradicate poverty and hunger through sustainable, values-based holistic community development. Heifer distributes animals, along with agricultural and values-based training, to families in need around the world as a means of providing self-sufficiency."[5]
EDUCATION	My biggest source of donation is education, because I believe education creates opportunity. Every year we take a portion of proceeds from our certifications and provide full and partial certification scholarships to women in need. Recipients include: women escaping domestic violence, reentering the workforce after having children, caring for loved ones with special needs, living with chronic illness or disabilities, displaced due to natural disasters, living in developing countries where high-quality health information is less accessible, and many more.

It isn't necessary to give to multiple charities, especially if you have a limited funds, but it's how I've chosen to support the various causes I care about.

You don't have to be purely altruistic with your financial choices either. Investing in women can be a wise financial choice as well as an incredible way to lift women up.

If you happen to be in a financial position to invest in business, consider diverse, women-run businesses. Savvy investors such as Arlan Hamilton of Backstage Capital have demonstrated the financial benefit of investing specifically in women-owned, People-of-Color-owned, and LGBTQIA+-owned startups. Arlan recently posted to Twitter, "I was asked if I'd be worried that I was missing 'the next Mark Zuckerberg' by not investing in straight, white men. Most investors should be asking themselves what if they miss the next tech icon by only investing in [straight, white men]."[5]

If you don't have the financial means to donate to organizations or have much choice in where you're able to spend your money, don't despair. Investing in yourself and your own financial health is one of the most powerful things you can do to help women in general rise up.

Your Superpowers Have a Ripple Effect

I might sound like a broken record here, but I can't stress this enough: small things add up.

Even driving an extra five minutes to support a women-owned coffee shop, making a fifteen-dollar monthly donation, scheduling a one-off mentoring chat, or participating in a once-yearly volunteer day can make a big difference.

That fifteen-dollar monthly donation adds up to nearly two hundred dollars by the end of the year. (Between 2012 and early 2020, Together Rising—one of my favorite charities—has raised over $25 million, with the most frequent donation of twenty-five dollars.[6])

One coffee date where you share insider knowledge with a new employee could give them the insight they need to excel. That single volunteer day can help a food bank get more meals in the hands of people who are hungry.

You never know how big your influence can be.

Next Steps

This chapter was all about using your superpowers to lift women up in ways that can make a big impact, while being true to you.

Below, you'll find exercises to guide you through creating your "superpower statement" similar to the one I shared in the beginning of this chapter. You can do these exercises immediately or return to these exercises once you've finished the book—whenever it's right for you.

To download your resource guide, visit:
www.MollyGalbraith.com/book-resources

Exercise #1: Create Your Superpower Statement

Step #1: Identify your top personal value from chapter 5.

Step #2: Determine why this is important to you.

When it comes to lifting women up, it can be helpful for us to get introspective and identify where our passion for helping women comes from. These are five of the most common origin paths we see at Girls Gone Strong. Check the box of the story that is most true to your path:

- ☐ I grew up helping people. It's something I've always done.
- ☐ I had a mentor or role model who changed my life, and now I want to pay it forward.
- ☐ I watched a woman in my life suffer, and I want to do whatever I can to help others who are suffering.

- ☐ I overcame personal challenges, and I don't want other women to have experiences like mine.
- ☐ I've struggled in my relationships with other women, and I'm ready to change that.
- ☐ I have other reasons (write them down).

Step #3: Get clear on your skills and talents.

The work of lifting women up can be done many different ways. Identifying your skills and talents can give you great insight on how you can do work that feels fun, exciting, and fulfilling.

Your talents and skills might not seem like they have anything to do with helping women. However, once you have identified them, you can learn how to use them to lift women up.

Ask yourself the following questions:

1. What talents or abilities or characteristics best describe me?

2. What type of work or projects or leisure activities get me excited—e.g. organizing, connecting, volunteering, problem-solving, educating, mentoring, planning, etc.?

3. What do people count on me for or ask for my help with?

4. What am I doing when other people say they're impressed with me?

5. What are the things I'm most passionate about?

6. What are my top goals for myself personally, for my family, career, and life?

Step #4: Learn more about your relationships with other women.

1. Which two to three women are you closest to in your life? Why are you closest to them?

2. Who are two to three women in your life that you admire and why? What have you learned from them already? What else can you learn from them?

3. When have you most enjoyed the time you were spending with other women? Where were you? What were you doing?

4. What do other women think you do really well? What do other women compliment you on?

5. Think about your three most recent interactions with women in your life (i.e., not strangers). What, if anything, was good about the interactions? What, if anything, wasn't good about the interactions? Can you think of a way you can lift one (or all) of these women up?

Step #5: Determine who you are passionate about helping.

Over the years, I've learned that getting extremely clear on which women you want to help and how you want to help them can bring needed clarity and direction.

Having this clarity and direction will allow you to invest your time, knowledge, skills, and resources in a way that leaves you feeling satisfied and proud with the work you do.

Consider which group of women you want to help most. If you don't see the group you want to help listed below, write it down.

- ☐ women who are in my community (e.g., geographical, religious, shared interests, online)
- ☐ women/girls who are younger than I am
- ☐ women who are older than I am

- ☐ women who are part of a marginalized group
- ☐ women who need pre- and postnatal support
- ☐ women who need peri- and postmenopausal support
- ☐ women who need support with nutrition and exercise
- ☐ women who need support in their political aspirations
- ☐ women who need support in their professional aspirations
- ☐ I'd like to help women who . . .

Then ask yourself:

1. Why do I want to help this group of women? What problems are they currently struggling with?

2. What kind of help do I want to provide? What solution(s) do I want to provide them with—e.g., coaching advice, mentoring, donating to their cause, volunteering time, etc.?

Step #6: Assess what resources you have access to that can be used to lift women up.

Rate your access to the following resources on a scale from 1 to 10 by checking the corresponding box below:

1 = none, 5 = just enough for myself, 10 = big surplus

Resource	1	2	3	4	5	6	7	8	9	10
TIME										
MONEY										
NETWORK/ CONNECTIONS										
KNOWLEDGE/ WISDOM										
SKILLS/TALENT										
INFLUENCE/ PLATFORM										

1. What resources have the highest numbers?

2. What resources have the lowest numbers?

3. If you were to combine your highest-ranked resources and your top value to help women, what could that look like? For example:

- If skills and knowledge are both a 9, you're most passionate about helping women who need pre- and postnatal support, and you value connection, you might consider supporting pre- and postnatal women for a living as a doula or a coach.
- If network/connections are a 9 and time is a 7, you're passionate about helping young professionals, and your highest value is education, you might help young women in your city get connected with strong, successful mentors.

Step #7: Write your superpower statement.

Now it's time to pull it all together. Write a statement that includes:

- who you're passionate about helping
- how you want to help them
- what resources you want to use to help them
- how it's aligned with your core value

Examples:

> "I'm passionate about using my skills and knowledge to help pre- and postnatal women stay safe, healthy, and strong, during and after pregnancy through nutrition and exercise coaching, which aligns with my top value of connection."
>
> —SANDRA

> "I plan to use my network, connections, and time to facilitate mentorships between young professionals and women with more experience to help young women access the knowledge they need to be successful in their careers."
>
> —ROBIN

Step #8: Consider how this will fit into your life.

Now that you have clarity on what you want to do, take a moment to consider how these activities will fit into your life. Please note, the following questions are intended to spark inspiration and give you ideas of how you can lift women up today and in the future.

Ask yourself:

1. Is this something I want to make into a career or something I want to do in my free time?

2. If I don't want to make this into a career, can I implement some of this in my current work? If so, how?

3. Can I also implement it in my personal life? If so, how?

CHAPTER 10

Becoming a Role Model and Making a Lasting Difference

The higher purpose of my life is not the song and dance or the acclaim, but to rise up, to pull up others and leave the world and industry a better place.

—VIOLA DAVIS

CHAPTER 10

Becoming a Role Model and Making a Lasting Difference

You are a role model.

That's right. A role model.

Whether you like it or not, your behavior is influencing the people around you—and you have the opportunity to use that influence for good. In fact, role modeling is one of the most powerful tools we have to effect change.

I was fortunate to have great female role models in my mom and both of my grandmothers. My grandmother Dollie was an endless example of support and compassion. She volunteered several days a week for decades, was the first AVOL Kentucky (a front-lines organization dedicated to ending HIV in the Commonwealth) volunteer in Lexington, and loved her Sunday mornings helping at the Community Kitchen. In 1989, she received Kentucky's Volunteer of the Year Award. My other grandmother, Gama, marched with Dr. Martin Luther King Jr., operated a free drop-in care center for at-risk kids called Grandma's Corner, started a letter-writing campaign to government officials about human trafficking in the early nineties, and more. And my mom was one of several cofounders of the Lexington Community Sanctuary Group, offering financial and legal assistance and even helping house El Salvadorian refugees seeking political asylum. She was also an active volunteer for the Rape Crisis Center for years, chairing the Board of Directors and organizing their Take Back the Night marches.

Essentially, I come from a family of activists who believed deeply in helping others. This experience made me appreciate not only the importance of activism but the vast spectrum of what positive action can look like. You don't have to be an activist to change the lives of girls and women. Simply by exhibiting strength, personal empowerment, or taking on the approach of "lifting other women up," you can do a world of good and create new opportunities for other women and girls.

Positive Female Role Models Are Especially Important for Young Girls

Let's talk about girls for a second. I've mainly focused on lifting women up in this book because, as a coach, the majority of my experience has been working with adults rather than kids.

But it's important to recognize that you can make a huge difference for the girls in your life—and for future generations.

A Dove survey showed that 79 percent of girls opt out of activities they enjoy because they don't like the way that their bodies look.[1] This means many young girls aren't raising their hand in class, running for class president, auditioning for the school play, or trying out for a sports team—just because they don't feel their bodies are good enough.

You can imagine how opting out of activities that are important to them—day after day, week after week, year after year—impacts girls' growth, skill development, and potential as human beings. These young girls are at a disadvantage before they even enter adulthood because their perceived not-enoughness prevents them from participating in activities that they love.

What if, instead of holding back, these girls were able to see and believe that:

- other girls are not their enemy
- they can be and do anything
- they can achieve as much success as their hearts desire
- someone else having an opportunity doesn't mean they can't get great opportunities too

If we want young girls to understand that strong girls lift other girls up, they must see us modeling what that looks like in our everyday lives.

Furthermore, aspiring to be a role model isn't just good for others—it's good for us too.

A sense of meaning and purpose is considered one of the five elements of well-being, as theorized by psychologist Martin Seligman, a leading researcher on what is known as positive psychology. Being a role model can give you that sense of meaning and purpose—a reason to get out of bed every morning or to show up as your best self in the face of challenges. In turn, this can ease stress and increase a sense of focus, confidence, and fulfillment.

How to Find Your Inner Role Model

Want to know how you can be an amazing role model for girls and women?

Start by being you.

That might seem like a fluffy strategy, but it's one of the most powerful things you can do.

One of *my* role models, Marie Forleo, always says, "The world needs that special gift that only you have." I couldn't agree more. By being yourself and tapping into your superpowers, you can do a world of good for young girls and other women who are watching and waiting for role models.

Think about all the incredible women you've been introduced to thus far in this book. They each changed so many lives through the ripple effects created when they chose to be themselves and use their superpowers.

For example, my massage therapist Taryn Chula was just being her loving, compassionate self when she showed me a different way of viewing women and my relationships with them and planted a seed in me that would eventually lead to the creation of GGS and this book.

Emily Ho was just being herself when she started her blog about her weight-loss journey and then opened up about the death of her mom and her struggles with binge eating disorder, anxiety, depression, and ADHD. Her work has continued to evolve as she herself has evolved, and now she inspires hundreds of thousands of women to feel seen and represented and get access to comfortable and stylish clothing that fits their bodies.

Chrissy King was just being herself and sharing her truth when she spoke up about the lack of representation of Black women, Women of Color, and body diversity in the health and fitness space. Her story resonated deeply with others, and now she's a leader in anti-racism and diversity, equity, and inclusion education in the health and fitness space. She helps other Black women and Women of Color understand that they belong and deserve to take up space in the health and wellness industry.

Janae Marie Kroczaleski was just being herself when she chose to share her story about being transgender, gender fluid, and nonbinary. She told her story through media, in a powerful documentary, and in her private conversations with friends and colleagues. Now people in her life and in the fitness industry as a whole have become more supportive of other LGBTQIA+ folks, and she's continuing to lead and inspire.

Taryn, Emily, Chrissy, and Janae are all amazing people (as are the many other women you've read about in previous chapters), but you're no different. How you're living your everyday life is positively impacting other people. Whether you're being a great parent, leading well in your workplace, volunteering your time, complimenting other women, or raising money for a good cause, others are watching and feeling inspired by what you do.

That's why we must remember that small actions can have an enormous impact—a ripple effect so powerful it's impossible to measure. For me, seeing the everyday small, quiet actions of others inspires me to take action in my life. And I'm here to tell you that your own actions, however small, can make change feel more accessible and possible to other women.

If you feel inspired to volunteer five days a week, create life-saving vaccines for children, or dedicate your life to eradicating poverty, that's awesome. But these aren't your only options for inspiring others.

Sometimes, in addition to being yourself, the most important thing you can do is keep showing up.

The Importance of Being There

> "I was 16 years old, saw her on television, got the inspiration to think, maybe I could do that. We all [fellow female journalists] recognize that had it not been for her, we would not have had a shoulder to stand on."[2]
>
> —OPRAH WINFREY, SPEAKING ABOUT HER ROLE MODEL, BARBARA WALTERS

Just by showing up, you can pave the way.

For starters, let's look at the workplace. There's evidence to suggest that when a woman is the only woman at her job, she has a more difficult work experience and is more inclined to leave that job or switch fields altogether.

Take the STEM fields. Women in STEM (science, technology, engineering, and mathematics) report constantly fighting against the sexist bias that they don't perform as well as men in the field, and many women leave the field because of it.[3]

However, when women in STEM have strong female role models, women not only stay in the field longer but perform better in their roles.

In other words, by staying in the field and doing their jobs, women in STEM help other women continue their careers and stay in the field too—all while doing fantastic work! As you can imagine, this has an exponential effect.

By the way, it is possible to increase female representation in a particular field. STEM industries have been notoriously low in female representation, but a number of organizations, businesses, governments, and individuals have been working to get more women and girls interested in STEM and keep them there. And guess what? Recent data shows it's paying off. A 2018 report from LinkedIn says that more women entered STEM in the past forty years than any other field.[4] This has taken years and a lot of groundwork, but it was possible. The things you do for women and your industry today could make a big difference for years to come.

Here's another example of how just being there can create a massive ripple effect—this time, from the world of sports.

For years, fencing was typically dominated by white men. Then, in 1972, Ruth White became the first African American female fencer to represent Team USA. More Women of Color followed in her footsteps, shifting the demographics of the sport.[5]

In 2016, Ibtihaj Muhammad became the first Muslim American woman to wear a hijab while competing for the United States in the Olympics. She also earned a bronze medal in the Rio Olympics as part of Team USA, becoming the first female Muslim American athlete to earn a medal at the Olympics.[6]

Her example has inspired many women to follow in her footsteps. Since Ibtihaj's example, the number of Muslim women competing in hijabs has continued to increase steadily.[7]

These are just a couple of examples of how you can be a game changer with your very presence.

I've seen this myself in the fitness industry. When I first started lifting weights in 2004, I was almost always the only woman in the weight room. Fast-forward to today, and depending on the gym you're in, women might make up 50 percent or more of the population in the weight room. This is due to a number of factors: more women are talking about weightlifting, participating in weightlifting, inviting other women to lift with them, posting about it on social media, and role modeling it for other women. Countless women have told me they got the confidence to walk into the weight room and start lifting because they saw other women in there or they saw a video online of a woman lifting.

Your presence matters to girls too. For example, evidence indicates that girls are more likely to be politically active if they're exposed to more women in politics. A study published in 2018 by researchers at the University of Colorado Boulder and Notre Dame found that prominent female political role models inspire other women to run for office.

"Researchers found that, on average, the presence of a female governor or U.S. senator in a state translated to an additional seven women running for state legislature in the next election cycle. The researchers also found evidence of a so-called 'legacy effect,' meaning that having a female governor or U.S. senator continued to have an impact on the number of women who ran for that state's legislature in subsequent years."[8]

The lesson here?

Get yourself in the places you want to be—and you want other women to be—and keep showing up!

Being There for the Women in Your Life Matters Too. Probably More Than You Think.

I learned this after my dad passed away unexpectedly in 2012.

My best friend Dr. Angela Gorrell was living in LA, working as a minister and going to school. Living in LA on a part-time minister's salary wasn't easy, but she made it work. She came to Kentucky for Christmas in December 2011 to visit her family and then flew back to LA on January 2.

On January 4, Angela got word that my dad had died. Her first instinct was to come and be with me, but she was concerned about the cost of the flight.

She called her mom (who's like a second mom to me) and asked, "Mom, what do I do?"

Her mom replied, "What's a best friend for if not to fly back to be by her best friend's side when her dad dies?"

So she put a $900 flight on her credit card and flew back to be with me.

Having her there meant everything to me. I couldn't have gotten through that time without her support.

Five years later, in January 2017, Angela's dad died. I didn't have to travel nearly as far, but you can bet I dropped everything and hit the road, driving to be with her and her sister Jenna in Cincinnati as soon as I heard the news.

On both occasions we just sat together—sometimes in silence, sometimes with tears streaming down our cheeks—bearing witness to each other's pain.

Dr. Brené Brown says, "An experience of collective pain does not deliver us from grief or sadness; it is a ministry of presence. These moments remind us that we are not alone in our darkness and that our broken heart is connected to every heart that has known pain since the beginning of time."[9]

Being together after our fathers died didn't take away the pain. But it was, and still is, one of the most sacred times of my life, and it taught me the importance of being there for other women when it matters most.

Playing the Long Game

Because humans are hardwired for survival, it's easy for our brains to get stuck in the here and now. The idea of a two-week jumpstart or a thirty-day challenge excites us. It's way less exciting for us to think about a thirty-year plan.

Just like health and fitness, lifting women up isn't just about what you do and the changes you make over the next week or month or even three months, although those changes are important. It's about making decisions and taking daily action that casts a vote in favor of who and what you want to become and the impact you want to have on the world. Yes, small actions can have powerful ripple effects, but *consistent* small actions create massive, sweeping change.

If you're a fan of analogies (I totally am), think of this concept in relation to your exercise or nutrition. Yes, eating a huge salad every day for fourteen days or going on a thirty-minute walk three times a week for a month are fantastic things to do for yourself and your health. But imagine if you did those things regularly for a year. Or five years. Or fifteen years. Imagine how those relatively small decisions would compound over time.

It's important to remember that anytime you try to implement new thoughts, words, and actions into your life, the process takes time. Old thoughts, words, and actions will try to creep back in. This is normal. Maybe you find yourself feeling jealous of another woman or you refrain from sharing insider knowledge with a coworker for fear that she'll get promoted over you or you gossip about a mutual acquaintance with one of your friends.

When this happens, I recommend using this simple three-step approach to recenter yourself:

Step #1: Notice, Name, and Normalize

Being aware of what's happening and not judging yourself for it allows you to recognize and take responsibility for it without wallowing in guilt or shame.

Step #2: Get Curious

Ask yourself, *What's going on in my life or in my brain right now that's leading me to feel this way?* And, *If I were being the best version of myself, what would I do?* These questions allow you to identify situations or people that might provoke these feelings and also help you figure out how to do better. Remember, this is like "Fake it 'til you make it," but better. Because it's not fake. It's authentic and true to who you are when you're being the best version of yourself.

Step #3: Take Action

Actions create habits, habits build skills, and the accumulation of skills ultimately leads to achieving goals (i.e., your version of success). Yet change and success are ongoing processes. You can't take one action, or make one attempt, and expect that you'll be good to go. It requires ongoing effort for new actions to become habitual behavior. And that's okay! You can do this. I believe in you. And I promise you that the changes you're making will create a better life for you and a better world for women and girls.

Bonus Step: Set Implementation Intentions

Implementation intentions are simply an "if/then" plan you make in advance about what you will do or how you will handle a situation: "If X happens, then I will do Y."

This is a powerful method we use in coaching to help our clients stay consistent with the habits and practices they need in order to reach their goals.

You can even add a "because" to the end of the implementation intention to remind yourself why this is important to you and make your intention even more powerful: "If X happens, then I will do Y *because* Z."

Some examples of what this strategy might look like for lifting other women up:

- If I find myself hesitant to praise my coworker in front of my boss, then I'll take a deep breath and do it anyway because I want to be a strong woman who lifts other women up.
- If my friend starts talking negatively about our mutual acquaintance, then I'll tell her I'd prefer to talk about something else because I'm not interested in gossiping about other women.
- If my friend texts me gushing about her new relationship and I feel jealous, then I'll pause for five minutes and text her back how excited I am for her because she is important to me and I really do want her to be happy.

Of course, despite your best intentions, you are going to make mistakes sometimes. Here's how to handle that.

How to Keep Going When You Make a Mistake

A huge part of being a role model is about how you deal with mistakes. In fact, your mistakes might be your best opportunities to be a role model for others.

We all make mistakes. It's how you deal with them that matters.

And if you're worried about making a mistake, I've got good news for you: you're definitely going to mess up.

You might be thinking, *Is that really good news, Molly?*

I know. It may sound terrifying. But if you avoid going after your dreams and doing what makes you happy because you're afraid of mistakes, guess what? You're going to make mistakes anyway. That's just how life is. So you can be worried, play small, and try to avoid screwing up at all costs—which is futile.

Or you can:

- go after your dreams
- do what makes you happy
- live in alignment with your own values and purpose
- feel good knowing you're living a life you're proud of
- create more opportunity and a better world for women and girls

Because of scarcity mindset, many women live in perpetual fear of what others may think. We pursue perfectionism and try to prevent our flaws from showing because we've been taught that, to get ahead or be accepted, we must be better than everyone else.

I lived like this for many years. Constantly worried about what other people thought of me. Shifting my self-worth based on what other people thought.

Then over time (and through lots of therapy), I stopped worrying about the imperfection of my actions and my life and my body, and I started concentrating on being the person I wanted to be: a woman who lifts other women up.

I started helping and celebrating other women rather than focusing on my own perceived weaknesses or flaws. That mindset shift changed everything. It was a huge relief because I finally was able to put all that perfectionism and fear aside and start living as the person I'm meant to be, according to the values I believe in.

It's not always easy. No one likes to make mistakes, especially when those mistakes hurt or disappoint other people, and it's not easy to admit your flaws or embrace your imperfections, even while you try to do better. When I realize I've made a big mistake, my heart races, my whole body flushes, and I get butterflies in my stomach. It takes time for me to calm down, center my thoughts, and figure out what to do next. It's hard, but messing up is part of the work of lifting women up.

If you're worried about messing up, here are some things you need to remember.

First of all, it's not about winning. Conversations these days—especially those on social media—can feel like competitions. Like it's up to us to prove others wrong and come out on top. But I've said before the goal isn't to "win" because there is no winning. There's only living true to your values, doing the best you can, and when you know better, you do better.

Second, there will always be people who are upset with you. Sometimes you'll make legitimate mistakes. And sometimes you'll do everything "right" and people will still be pissed off with you. You're going to do things people don't agree with and have different opinions about. That's a fact of life.

But what's the alternative? As the Elbert Hubbard quote goes: "To escape criticism, say nothing, do nothing, be nothing."[10]

If we accept that some degree of criticism is inevitable, I think it makes it easier to drop our defenses and think critically about our own actions.

If you get criticized or called out, you might consider: *Did I really mess up here? Is there an actual problem, or are there just different perspectives on how this should be handled? Do I owe someone an apology?*

Of course, when you make a mistake, it's natural to go into defense mode, to try to protect yourself. For many of us (including me), that process goes like this:

Shame and Defensiveness Spiral

Realize (or get told) we've made a mistake

↓

Immediately feel shame and defensiveness

↓

Start explaining why it happened

↓

Secretly wonder what we could have done better or beat ourselves up for how much we suck

Defense mode doesn't serve us. Instead—and this is tricky, I admit—the best thing you can do after making a mistake is to take full responsibility.

This can seem counterintuitive, but when you shirk responsibility, blame others, or completely defend your actions, you're stepping out of your power. You're relinquishing your ability to own your actions, learn from them, and make new decisions going forward.

But if you step up and say, "Yep, I did that thing, my mistake," you stand in your own power. By starting with self-responsibility, you approach that mistake or problem from a place that allows you to learn and grow.

Once you've taken responsibility, apologize. Acknowledge the harm you caused. Then commit to doing better.

Choosing to grow from our mistakes is a huge gift to ourselves. It invites compassion and self-acceptance as well as an opportunity to grow stronger and continue striving for our biggest dreams with the security of knowing we can accept our failures and missteps along the way.

Similarly, helping others do better is part of lifting other women up.

Ignoring a mistake is often the easiest path, but it's not the most helpful, compassionate, or loving approach. If we're going to do better together, we need to hold one another accountable, challenge one another to do better, and educate one another. It can be uncomfortable to hold others accountable, and to be held accountable ourselves, but it's the best way for all of us to grow and create the sort of lives we want for ourselves and the world we want to live in.

What Will People Think?

If you've ever worried about doing something for fear of what others might think, you're not alone. When I was a little girl, I'd go crying to my mom about something mean someone had said about me. "Mom! Allison called me a baby!"

My mom would comfort me briefly, and then she'd look at me and say, "Well, *are* you a baby?" and I'd stick out my lower lip and furrow my little brow and say, "No." And she would say, "Well, alright then. It's settled. What Allison thinks doesn't matter. It's what *you* think of *you*. That's it. It's all you, sweet girl."

While my mom did a good job modeling this for me, I still have these fears on occasion, and when I do, I like to draw strength from other powerful, untamed women.

> "It took me until my late thirties to understand that I can't make someone like me. I can't dictate how someone views me or what that person views as fact versus fiction when it comes to my life."[11]
>
> —ARLAN HAMILTON

> "We are not what other people say we are. We are who we know ourselves to be, and we are what we love. That's okay."[12]
>
> —LAVERNE COX

> "Whether you are brave or not cannot be judged by people on the outside. Sometimes being brave requires letting the crowd think you're a coward. Sometimes being brave means letting everyone down but yourself."[13]
>
> —GLENNON DOYLE
>
> "Staying true to who you are moment to moment is a radical act of self-love that absolutely cannot be married to needing other people's approval."[14]
>
> —ELIZABETH DIALTO
>
> "Barack and I, all through our presidency, through the lies and the stuff they said about us . . . all we could do was wake up every day and do our jobs and let our jobs and our lives speak for ourselves."[15]
>
> —MICHELLE OBAMA

Always Enough, Never Enough

There's a saying I try to live by: "Always enough, never enough." It's shorthand for the idea that what I'm doing is good enough, yet at the same time, I can always do better.

The first part of the saying means that when I try my best, given the knowledge, skills, and resources I have at the time, I need to accept that's good enough and not beat myself up about not being perfect or not doing everything. Perfectionism is a quick path to misery, and we're only human. This core belief also allows me to extend the space and grace to others to make mistakes.

The second half is equally important. It means there's always room for improvement. All of us can do better, always. That drive to improve is what moves us each forward. It's what keeps us growing as people, and collectively, it's what keeps us moving forward as groups, communities, and societies.

These two ideas may seem contradictory, but they're more of a paradox:

two things that, while they may seem in opposition, are both true. This paradox gives me the peace to accept myself as I am, where I am, while also accepting that I can and must always do better and be better.

On my journey, other people have been instrumental in helping me become a better person and leader by pointing out my mistakes or failings; calling me in, out, or up to do better; or showing me ways I can improve.

This hasn't always felt good, but ultimately, I'm grateful for these people.

As a reminder of something I stated early in the book, "Strong women lift each other up" doesn't mean we always back what all women do 100 percent. Sometimes, lifting each other up means challenging one another to rethink the way we're doing things, or challenging one another to be better. It also means giving others the grace and acknowledgment that we're all usually doing the best we can at that moment.

In that way, "Always enough, never enough" isn't just a personal mantra—it's a way of working with other women too. When you apply this idea to your life and interactions with others, you'll find amazing personal growth—and you'll challenge others to do better too.

I'll be honest: as I've written this book, I've been a bit uncomfortable at times. It feels a little weird to be the one holding the microphone, championing the idea of lifting others up while writing my own book.

Even with everything I've shared here, I still have my own weaknesses and shortcomings—and I always will.

And that's okay.

Let's be real. Sometimes you may feel inspired, empowered, and excited about the impact you're able to make. Other times you may wonder whether you're doing enough.

The answer will be yes and no.

This in-between, imperfect, messy tension is not only part of the process but also precisely where the magic happens.

Luckily, no matter where you are in your journey, you won't be alone. Because when you lift other women up, after a while, you discover there's always someone there to lift you up too.

Next Steps

This chapter was all about how you can further the mission of being a strong woman who lifts other women up by being a role model for other women and girls.

Below you'll find questions that will help you think deeply about how you've been impacted by role models in your life, both positively and negatively, and get clear on who you want to be a role model for, how you're already being a role model, and how you can keep learning and growing to continue creating a better future for women and girls.

You can do these exercises immediately or return to these exercises once you've finished the book—whenever it's right for you.

To download your resource guide, visit:
www.MollyGalbraith.com/book-resources

Exercise #1: How Role Models Have Impacted You

1. Who has been a role model for you? Think of one to three women and write them below.

Remember, they don't have to be the first woman to go to the moon or end world hunger to be a role model (although those are great role models to have!). Your role model could be someone you know or don't know. They could be in your line of work or involved in a hobby you're interested in. They could be a stranger you witnessed speaking up in a difficult situation or a coworker who refuses to engage in gossip.

2. How did they help you, or what difference did that make in your life?

3. Who in your life has role modeled behavior you don't want to emulate?

For example, maybe you had a boss who didn't treat you well, a teacher who used shame to discipline you, or a mom with whom you don't have a strong relationship and you want to be a different kind of mother to your kids.

Exercise #2: How You Can Impact Others through Role Modeling

1. Who would you like to be a role model for? Your kids? Your employees? Your students? Female entrepreneurs? Women in your community or at your gym?

2. Are there ways you think you're already a good role model for these women and girls?

3. What are some ways you can use your superpowers you've learned about in this book to be a role model for women and girls *in the future*?

4. What are some ways you can be a role model for women and girls right away—e.g., catch your friend doing something right, give your coworker credit in your next meeting, give your daughter or niece a genuine compliment on something other than her body, speak up next time your sister gossips about another woman, etc.?

5. Now it's time to take action! Choose one or two things you're going to do as soon as you set this book down to lift other women up. Be specific. Say what you're going to do, and when and for whom you're going to do it—e.g., as soon as I put this book down, I'm going to call my best friend and tell her how much I appreciated her being there for me when I went through my terrible breakup/death of a loved one/lost job/etc.).

Conclusion

What if instead of longing for ease, we were made for more—made to advocate, made to dig in, made to speak out, made to dive into nuance, made for complexity, made for this moment. . . . What if we believed so deeply in our own capacity to rise to this occasion that getting to work wasn't a tiring chore, but a life-giving opportunity to invest in something larger than ourselves?

—AUSTIN CHANNING BROWN

Conclusion

As I wrap up writing this book, I've been reflecting on all the women who have lifted me up in the course of my life. The women whose stories you just read about, and so many more who inspired, taught, and supported me. Their effect on me has been immeasurable.

Of course, it's not just the women who've been directly involved in my life whom I have to thank. It's all the women who've helped create the world we live in, and the opportunities that we do have.

In the United States, it wasn't that long ago that women were lacking opportunity in even bigger ways. It wasn't that long ago that unmarried women couldn't access birth control, women couldn't open up a bank account without their husband's signature, couldn't get a law degree, couldn't attend a desegregated school . . . the examples go on and on.

While we have a long way to go, it's undeniable that we've made progress throughout the course of history.

So how did we get here? How did we make the progress we've made? If you look back, it's because of the women who've paved the way.

Women like Rosa Parks, Betty Friedan, Gloria Steinem, Angela Davis, Marsha P. Johnson, Sylvia Rivera, Fannie Lou Hamer, Ruby Bridges, Ruth Bader Ginsburg, Delores Huerta, and Wilma Mankiller

and

. . . all the women whose stories have been erased or ignored because of racism, colorism, transphobia, ableism, and other forms of systemic injustice

and

. . . even more women who didn't make the history books, not just because women are often excluded from written history, but because great change often comes from small, unhistorical, yet crucial action.

Collectively, whether properly celebrated or not, the women who've come before us are the reason we've made the progress we've made. They each took steps to lift other women up. They marched. They donated. They campaigned. They wrote letters. They went to school. They ran for office. They applied for jobs. They started companies. They stood their ground. They used their voices. They told their stories. They supported one another. And hundreds more efforts that can never really be captured by historians, because they're too mundane or too small or there were simply too many to count. But every effort made a difference.

They probably couldn't see it at the time, but each of the efforts these women made had a lasting ripple effect—an incalculable difference to other women and, ultimately, society at large.

We can be part of this legacy. And we need to be, because we can't take for granted that the world will become better in the future. We have to create it ourselves.

That means we must choose. We must choose to lift women up in our everyday lives. If we commit to doing that, and we ensure that our commitment extends to *all* women (not just a few), and we work together . . . well, then we can make a ripple effect so big that the next generation of girls will live in a world far better than what we grew up in.

To create that kind of change, we need a lot of things. We need women donating and mentoring and supporting and educating. We need women signing petitions and marching and protesting. We need women innovating and inventing and researching; we need women leading organizations and running for office and making beautiful art and fighting for access and showing up at work day to day; and we need women who are birthing and raising and teaching the next generation of powerful girls.

We need women who are crediting and amplifying other women, hiring them and buying from them and making sure they're getting paid equitably; women who are raising their voices and having hard conversations and calling people in and holding one another accountable; women who are building bigger tables and claiming their space and making the bold, audacious choice to be themselves.

We need every single one of these things and more if we are going to create massive change and opportunity for women. We need every single woman to do the things she's good at and that she loves to do and that lights her on fire.

In other words, we need *you*.

We need you to help carry forward the legacy that all those amazing women have laid for us.

If there's one thing I hope you take away from this book, it's that change has to come from the top-down, the bottom-up, the outside-in, and the inside-out. And we need all different kinds of efforts and involvement to make an impact, and no act is too small. Just like all the women before you, every single action you take is a vote in favor of who you want to be, and the kind of world you want to create.

So the question becomes: What kind of world do you want to see?

I don't know about you, but I want to see a world where women aren't told they have to live in scarcity, where they aren't told, "There's not enough opportunity for you."

I want to see a world where women believe they're enough just as they are.

And I want to see a world where women feel happy to see other women succeed.

Because we know the more women who are thriving, the better we all are.

What about you?

Do you want to be part of a culture where we know that lighting another woman's candle doesn't dim or detract from our own flame? A culture where our flames spread like wildfire, lighting the path for the women who come after us?

Do you want to see a world where women—all women—are equitably represented and recognized in business and in government and in boardrooms and in all of the spaces and places where important decisions are made?

Do you want to live in a world where women aren't fighting one another for their rightful seat at the table, but are actively engaged in building bigger tables and inviting all of our sisters to sit with us?

This is the kind of world we're building, step by step.

Together we can make it happen, one strong woman at a time.

Thank you for being part of this journey with me. I can't wait to see the paths you blaze.

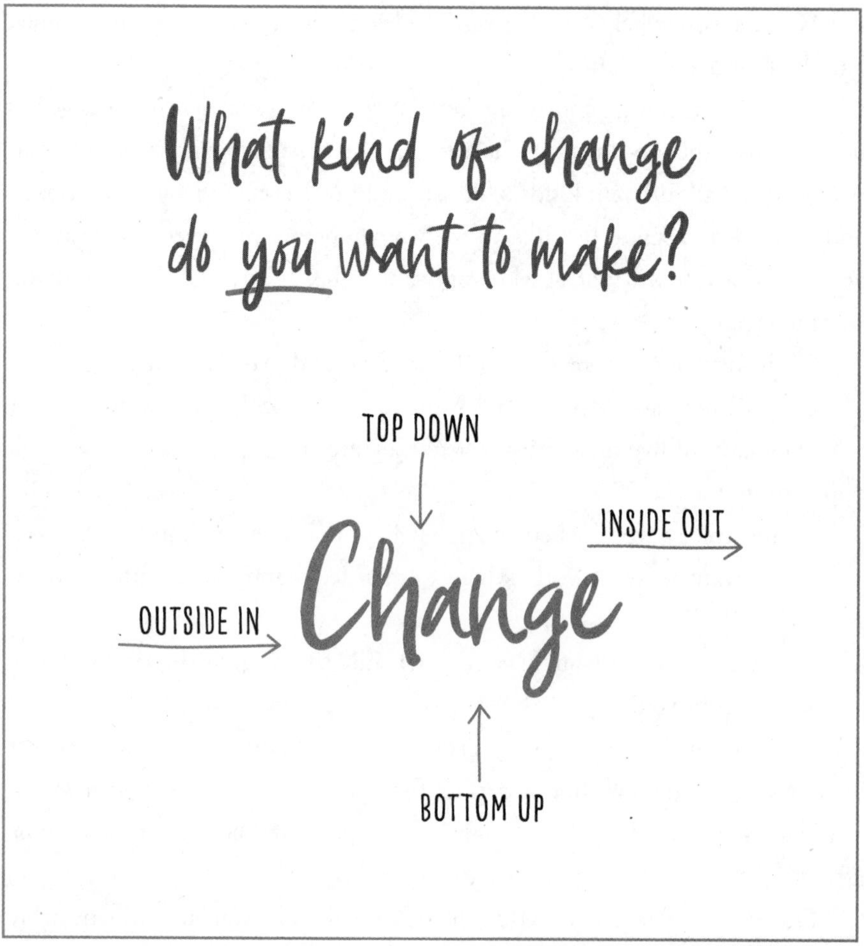

What kind of change do *you* want to make?

TOP DOWN

INSIDE OUT

OUTSIDE IN

Change

BOTTOM UP

How I Wrote This Book

This book is creative nonfiction, defined as "writing that uses literary styles and techniques to create factually accurate narratives."[1]

Throughout this book, I share my story and the stories of many other women. The stories of other women came from direct interviews, cited sources, or from my own memory.

In the instances they come from direct interviews or my memory, I invited as many people as I could to review their story, to ensure it's as factually accurate as possible.

In every instance, I have told the truth as I remember it, to the best of my ability, while fully aware other folks may have different memories or perspectives of particular events.

I've also been heavily influenced by the teachings of countless women, some whose names I remember, and others whose names I don't. I've done my best to credit these women, to whom I'm very grateful. My ideas are an amalgamation of their teachings, my research, my lived experiences, and my vision for the kind of world I want to see.

Quick Note From Me

No matter what brought you here—or what your exact interests are—there's something I want you to know . . .

I believe in you.

In your ability to be strong, to achieve your goals, and to make a difference . . . while lifting other women up along the way.

I'm honored you've chosen to spend your time with me. Thanks for being here.

xoxo,
Molly

P.S. If you enjoyed this book, please consider leaving a review.

Positive reviews help more women find this book and ultimately help drive our mission forward and lift more women up.

If you'd like to leave a review, simply visit the link below. Thanks in advance for taking the time to do this—I'm very grateful.

Leave a review:
www.MollyGalbraith.com/book-review

Remember to download your Companion Resource Guide:
www.MollyGalbraith.com/book-resources

Reference Guide to Exercises, Charts, Tables, and Other Important Resources

Ready to take your next steps?

I've compiled a checklist of all the thought exercises, charts, tables, and other important information in *Strong Women Lift Each Other Up* for quick reference. This will allow you to quickly find information you're looking for, or easily share a concept you really enjoyed with a friend.

And don't forget—you can download printable and fillable PDF versions of all the exercises here:

> Find more here: www.MollyGalbraith.com/book-resources

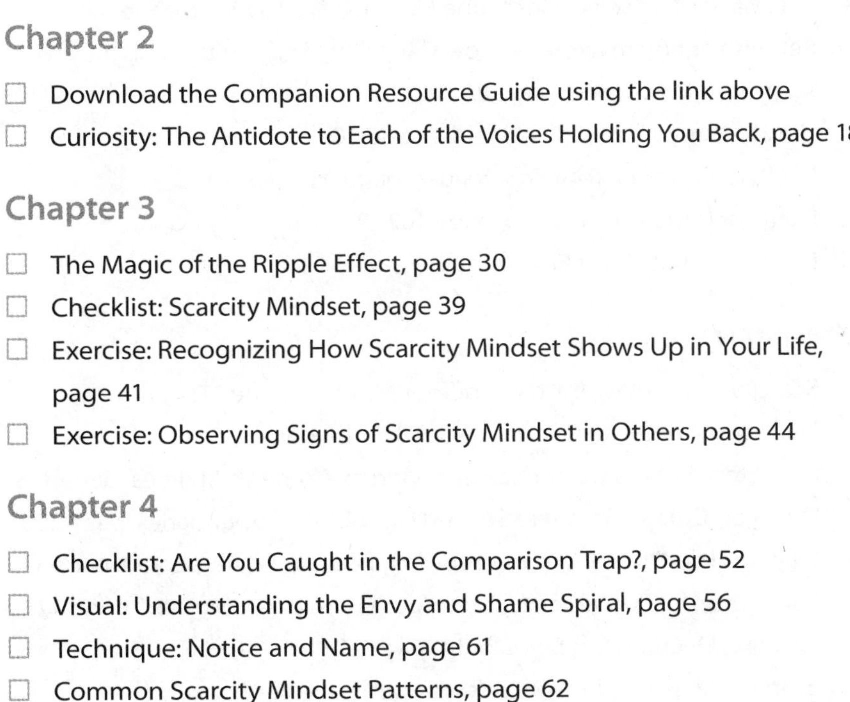

Chapter 5

Chapter 6

Chapter 7

- ☐ Molly's Process for Calling Someone In, page 161
- ☐ Exercise: Share Another Woman's Work, Idea, or Creation, page 167
- ☐ Exercise: Give Another Woman a Genuine Compliment, page 167
- ☐ Exercise: Catch Another Woman Doing Something Right, page 168
- ☐ Exercise: Give a Woman Credit Where Credit Is Due, page 168
- ☐ Exercise: Be Intentional in Your Spending, page 168
- ☐ Exercise: Endorse or Recommend Another Woman's Work, page 169
- ☐ Exercise: Speak Up When You Hear Something Negative Said About Another Woman, page 169
- ☐ Exercise: Consider Calling Someone In, page 169

Chapter 8

- ☐ Four-Step Process for Handling Negative Comments, page 178
- ☐ The "Good News" Ripple Effect, page 184
- ☐ How to Express Joy When You're Feeling Less Than Joyful, page 185
- ☐ Four Ways You Can Help Women Be Fully Heard in Any Environment, page 191
- ☐ Five Tips for Learning How to Say No, page 196
- ☐ Exercise: Share your Story, page 199
- ☐ Exercise: Respond to Criticism, page 201
- ☐ Exercise: Share Your Good News, page 202
- ☐ Exercise: Celebrate Other Women's Good News, page 202
- ☐ Exercise: Help Other Women Get Their Voices Heard, page 203
- ☐ Exercise: Say No the Right Way, page 205
- ☐ Exercise: Recover from Saying the Wrong Thing, page 207

Chapter 9

- ☐ Mentoring, Teaching, and Sharing Insider Knowledge, page 216
- ☐ Six Tips for Hiring Women and Creating Diverse Teams, page 221
- ☐ Three Steps to Start Donating and Investing, page 230
- ☐ Exercise: Create Your Superpower Statement, page 233

Chapter 10

Gratitudes

"Better together" isn't just a cute motto—it's a way of living and doing and being. Every great and meaningful thing I've ever done has been connected to other people. This book is the culmination of decades of being inspired, encouraged, helped, led, and loved by others, to whom I'm very grateful.

Family

To my beloved business and life partner, Casey—you have a nearly impossible job, yet you show up every day and do it anyway. You always know how to pull the best out of me, and this book is better because of you. Thank you for loving me, believing in me, and being (or becoming) good at everything I'm not good at. I love living an unconventional life with you.

To my dad, Gatewood—you showed me what it looks like to speak truth to power, to have a vision for a better world, and to pursue it relentlessly. Thank you for always, always telling me how proud you were of me. I miss you so much it hurts.

To my mom, Susan—you are one of the greatest influences of my life. Thank you for loving me and for understanding the sacrifices I make to do the work I was put here to do. Your support means everything to me. I love you more than the sun and the moon and the stars in the sky, and I love being your favorite youngest daughter. Thank you also for bringing Bill into my life.

To my sister Summer—I appreciate you, admire you, love you, trust you, and have so much fun with you. I love how our relationship has evolved. You are one of my best friends. Thank you also for bringing Kate and Ella into my life.

To my sister Abby—so much of your life was spent loving, caring for, and protecting me, and for that I am forever grateful. Our bond runs deep. You're the only person in the world I can exchange one glance with and know exactly what they're thinking, and I love that about us. And thank you for making me an aunt; Connor brings me so much joy. I love you.

To my grandmothers, Dollie and Helen (Gama)—you were two of the strongest women I've ever known. I was (and am) deeply inspired by your commitment to serving others, particularly those marginalized by society. Dollie, I'll forever treasure our Sunday brunches at Perkins with Dad and the family. And Gama, I loved our summers together doing math workbooks, and our biweekly dates at Sayre, painting, coloring, and doing (even more!) math together. I love you and miss you both dearly.

Friends

To Angela—my best friend for nearly twenty-five years. You flew back across the country at a moment's notice when you found out my dad died. That's who you are . . . who you've always been. You taught me the importance of showing up for people you love, and intentionally investing in relationships that are important to you, and I'm a better friend and human because of you. You and Jenna are like sisters to me. I love you both.

To Jen, Ivonne, and Amber—where do I begin? The laughs, the cries, the stress, the freakouts, the fun, the joys, the triumphs, the growth . . . we've been through so much together. Thank you for helping me feel seen and known and loved, and for embodying everything this book is about. You inspire me.

To Emily and Sarah—my college roommates and dear friends: between the sorority events, the road trips, the clubs, the boys, the late nights, and the spring breaks, there are so many stories we could tell, but we never will. We grew up together, and I will treasure our memories forever.

To Meaghan and Haley—whether I show up at your doorstep to sleep on your couch after leaving a six-year relationship, or you show up at my doorstep with vegetable lasagna after my Dad dies unexpectedly—you two have always loved and cared for me when I needed you most. Thank you for not letting time and distance separate our hearts.

To Dustyn—you, my friend, are a badass. Whether it's graduating top of your law school class, making partner, being a loving wife and mother, or being a wonderful friend, you achieve excellence in all you do. And I love that no matter how long it's been, we can always pick up right where we left off.

To Allison P.—thank you so much for all the howling, knee-slapping, can't-catch-our-breaths-from-laughing breakfast and dinner dates we've had throughout the years. You are a good friend to me, and I miss you.

To Amanda G.—six years ago you opened your home and life to me and Casey and changed the course of our lives forever. Thank you for your friendship and continued support, and to you, JB, and the kids for making us feel like part of your family.

To Allison T.—I deeply admire the way you show up for yourself, your friends, and the things you believe in. You are fierce, tender, clear, kind, and *hilarious*. Thanks for always being a phone call away.

To Melissa—you have shown up for me over and over again in our friendship; in the front row of my presentation, in encouraging text messages, as an early mentor teaching me the ropes of traditional publishing, as an endorser for my book proposal, and in your unwavering support of me and this book. I am grateful to you and for you.

To Colene—I'm so glad Debra said we just "had to know each other." She was right. You are magic. You make me laugh, you make me think, and you *always* lead from the front. Thank you for being my teacher and friend.

To Chrissy—I love how deeply connected our stories and growth are becoming. The ripple effect you've created by lifting women up and using your voice and gifts in service of yourself and others inspires me. Thank you for being my friend.

To Alison, Jonathan, and Jessi—you three showed me the importance of community and chosen family in my life. Thank you for loving and supporting me. There's no one else I'd rather ride four-wheelers to El Chivo with.

To Rachel—thanks for saying yes to moving in with me the first night we met. I knew instantly you were my kind of person and would be a forever friend. I love watching you blaze trails; Lord knows *you are not done yet*. You and "Uncle" Stu are some of the best roommates Casey and I could hope for.

To my fellow Girls Gone Strong cofounders—Alli, Neghar, Julia, Marianne, Jen, and Nia—our collective passion to help women find their own strength changed the course of my life and the fitness industry forever, and I'm so grateful to each of you for that. Thank you for your continued love and support of me and GGS. You all are very special to me.

People Who Helped Make This Book Possible

To my friend, writing partner, and magnificent storyteller, Camille DePutter—thank you for guiding me, challenging me, and helping me share my vision and ideas with the world in a compelling way. You have a true gift and have helped me create something I'm deeply proud of. This book wouldn't have been the same without you. I am grateful.

To the GGS team—the most loving, supportive, authentic humans I know, including Alex, Amber, Austin, Carolina, Cody, Elizabeth, Fabi, Grace, Ivonne, Jen, Jo, Kelsey, Kimberly, Marika, Robin, Sandra, Sarah, Summer, and Tehani—I couldn't do *any* of the work I do without each of you. You are rock stars, and I'm the luckiest woman in the world to have you all by my side.

To Amy—thank you for your help in the early stages of this project. I appreciate you.

To the powerful women I interviewed for this book—thank you for allowing me to share the magic of your stories to inspire other women as you have inspired me.

To my mentor and dear friend Dr. John Berardi—thank you for sharing countless hours of your hard-earned wisdom with Casey and me, and for believing in this book enough to introduce me to your agent, Scott.

To Scott Hoffman and Jan Baumer, my wonderful agents—I cannot tell you how good it feels to have your wisdom and guidance as I walk through this wild process. Thank you for believing in me and my ideas.

To the Harper Horizon team, including Andrea Fleck-Nisbet, Amanda Bauch, and John Andrade—thank you for seeing and believing in our vision, trusting our team's talents, and for being the best publishing partners I could ever ask for.

To Sarah Williamson, Grace Cline, Jeremy Kramer, Julie Long, and Belinda Bass—thank you also for helping me create a book cover I'm so proud of.

To Sarah—thank you also for designing such a beautiful book interior, and for staying up until all hours of the night with me making sure it was perfect. And for working with Michael and the Digital Brew team to get the illustrations just right. Your thoughtful work made this book better.

To Taryn Chula—thank you for being a beacon of light in my life when I needed it most. The ripple effect of your words and actions is immeasurable.

Notes

Chapter 1: How Lifting Women Up Changed My Life

1. Stephen Miller, "Black Workers Still Earn Less Than Their White Counterparts," SHRM, June 11, 2020, https://www.shrm.org/resourcesandtools/hr-topics/compensation/pages/racial-wage-gaps-persistence-poses-challenge.aspx.
2. Alisha Haridasani Gupta, "Women, Burdened with Unpaid Labor, Bear Brunt of Global Inequality," *New York Times*, January 23, 2020, https://www.nytimes.com/2020/01/23/us/unpaid-work-economy-davos.html.
3. Clare Coffey et al., Time to Care: Unpaid and Underpaid Care Work and the Global Inequality Crisis, Oxfam International, January 2020, https://assets.oxfamamerica.org/media/documents/FINAL_bp-time-to-care-inequality-200120-en.pdf.
4. "National Studies," Stop Street Harassment, April 2019, http://www.stopstreetharassment.org/our-work/nationalstudy/.
5. "2018 Study on Sexual Harassment and Assault," Stop Street Harassment, http://www.stopstreetharassment.org/our-work/nationalstudy/2018-national-sexual-abuse-report/.
6. "Violence Against Women," World Health Organization, November 29, 2017, https://www.who.int/news-room/fact-sheets/detail/violence-against-women.

Chapter 2: Laying the Foundation

1. "Kimberlé Crenshaw on Intersectionality, More Than Two Decades Later," Columbia Law School, June 8, 2017, https://www.law.columbia.edu/news/archive/kimberle-crenshaw-intersectionality-more-two-decades-later.
2. Maria Godoy, "'Tiny Habits' Are the Key to Behavioral Change," NPR, February 27, 2020, https://www.npr.org/2020/02/25/809256398/tiny-habits-are-the-key-to-behavioral-change.

Chapter 3: Disrupting Scarcity Mindset

1. Jess Huang et al., "Women in the Workplace 2019," McKinsey & Company, October 15, 2019, https://www.mckinsey.com/featured-insights/gender-equality/women-in-the-workplace-2019.
2. Emma Hinchliffe, "The Number of Female CEOs in the Fortune 500 Hits an All-Time Record," *Fortune*, May 18, 2020, https://fortune.com/2020/05/18/women-ceos-fortune-500-2020/.

3. Dominic-Madori Davis, "One of the Only 4 Black Fortune 500 CEOs Just Stepped Down—Here Are the 3 That Remain," Business Insider, July 21, 2020, https://www.businessinsider.com/there-are-four-black-fortune-500-ceos-here-they-are-2020-2.
4. Peter Bodin, Francesca Lagerberg, and Kim Schmidt, *Women in Business: Building a Blueprint for Action* (London: Grant Thornton International, 2019), 2.
5. Kate Clark, "US VC Investment in Female Founders Hits All-Time High," TechCrunch, December 9, 2019, https://techcrunch.com/2019/12/09/us-vc-investment-in-female-founders-hits-all-time-high/.
6. "Women in the U.S. Congress 2020," Rutgers, https://cawp.rutgers.edu/women-us-congress-2020.
7. *Women in National Governments Around the Globe: Fact Sheet* (Washington, DC: Congressional Research Service, 2019), 1.
8. "Women in Government: Quick Take," Catalyst, August 18, 2020, https://www.catalyst.org/research/women-in-government/.
9. Sut Jhally, *Killing Us Softly 4* (Northampton, MA: Media Education Foundation, 2010).
10. A 2011 study suggested that people experience feelings of social rejection similarly to how they experience physical pain. See Ethan Kross et al., "Social Rejection Shares Somatosensory Representations with Physical Pain," *Proceedings of the National Academy of Sciences of the United States of America* 108, no. 15 (April 2011): 6270–75, https://doi.org/10.1073/pnas.1102693108.

Chapter 4: Overcoming Comparison and Jealousy

1. See Jiyoung Chae, "Explaining Females' Envy Toward Social Media Influencers," *Media Psychology* 21, no. 2 (June 2017): 246–62, https://doi.org/10.1080/15213269.2017.1328312; Dian A. de Vries, Helen G. M. Vossen, and Paulien van der Kolk–van der Boom, "Social Media and Body Dissatisfaction: Investigating the Attenuating Role of Positive Parent–Adolescent Relationships," *Journal of Youth and Adolescence* 48 (March 2019): 527–36, https://doi.org/10.1007/s10964-018-0956-9; Marika Tiggemann et al., "The Effect of Instagram 'Likes' on Women's Social Comparison and Body Dissatisfaction, *Body Image* 26 (September 2018): 90–97, https://doi.org/10.1016/j.bodyim.2018.07.002; and Philippe Verduyn et al., "Do Social Network Sites Enhance or Undermine Subjective Well-Being? A Critical Review," *Social Issues and Policy Review* 11, no. 1 (January 2017): 274–302, https://doi.org/10.1111/sipr.12033.
2. "Time Flies: U.S. Adults Now Spend Nearly Half a Day Interacting with Media," Nielsen, July 31, 2018, https://www.nielsen.com/us/en/insights/article/2018/time-flies-us-adults-now-spend-nearly-half-a-day-interacting-with-media/.
3. Shanna Hocking, "Why Are Women Expected to Work Like They Don't Have Children and Mother Like They Don't Work?," Motherly, accessed November 3,

2020, https://www.mother.ly/work/why-are-women-expected-to-work-like-they-dont-have-children-and-mother-like-they-dont-work.

4. Ali Wong, "Ali Wong Would Appreciate It If You Never Asked Her This Again," *Elle*, October 10, 2019, https://www.elle.com/culture/celebrities/a29389245/ali-wong-wants-whats-best-for-you/.
5. Rui Fan et al., "The Minute-Scale Dynamics of Online Emotions Reveal the Effects of Affect Labeling," *Nature Human Behavior* 3 (January 2019): 92–100, https://doi.org/10.1038/s41562-018-0490-5; Jared B. Torre and Matthew D. Lieberman, "Putting Feelings into Words: Affect Labeling as Implicit Emotion Regulation," *Emotion Review* 10, no. 2 (April 2018): 116–24, https://doi.org/10.1177/1754073917742706.
6. Melissa Urban, "Imposter Syndrome + What Judgment Is Really About," *Do the Thing* (podcast), July 2, 2019, https://whole30.com/podcast/10/dear-melissa-july2/.

Chapter 5: Living True to Yourself

1. Kirstyn Brown, "'I'm Not Interested in Changing How My Body Looks," *trong Fitness Magazine*, February 29, 2016, https://www.strongfitnessmag.com/motivation/get-inspired/mollygalbraith/.
2. Molly Galbraith (@mollymgalbraith), ""This is my body. This is not a before picture. This is not an after picture," Facebook, January 1, 2016, https://www.facebook.com/mollymgalbraith/photos/a.140617146061704.25312.137577139699038/802956603161085/.
3. Bronnie Ware, "Regrets of the Dying," *Bronnie Ware* (blog), https://bronnieware.com/blog/regrets-of-the-dying/.
4. Denis Metev, "How Much Time Do People Spend on Social Media?," Review 42, July 4, 2020, https://review42.com/how-much-time-do-people-spend-on-social-media/.
5. All content in Jameela's section not cited directly is adapted from her website, as of mid-2020: https://iweighcommunity.com.
6. BUILD Series, "Jameela Jamil's 'I Weigh' Activism Platform Is All About Embracing Who You Are," YouTube video, 0:15, September 26, 2019, https://www.youtube.com/watch?v=O4-iMv0E58M.
7. BUILD Series.
8. Allison Tenney, "Beyond Coaching," accessed November 3, 2020, https://allisontenneyfitness.com/about/.
9. Allison Tenney.
10. Sonja R. Price Herbert, "Black Girl Pilates: My Catalyst for Strength," Girls Gone Strong, accessed November 3, 2020, https://www.girlsgonestrong.com/blog/articles/black-girl-pilates-catalyst-strength/.

Chapter 6: Better Together

1. Katelyn M. Cooper, Anna Krieg, and Sara E. Brownell, "Who Perceives They Are Smarter? Exploring the Influence of Student Characteristics on Student Academic Self-Concept in Physiology," *Advances in Physiology Education* 42, no. 2 (June 2018): 200–208, https://doi.org/10.1152/advan.00085.2017.
2. Amrisha Vaish, Tobias Grossmann, and Amanda Woodward, "Not All Emotions Are Created Equal: The Negativity Bias in Social-Emotional Development," *Psychological Bulletin* 134, no. 3 (May 2008): 383–403, https://doi.org/10.1037/0033-2909.134.3.383.
3. Luis Carretié et al., "Emotion, Attention, and the 'Negativity Bias,' Studied Through Event-Related Potentials," *International Journal of Psychophysiology* 41, no. 1 (May 2001): 75–85, https://doi.org/10.1016/S0167-8760(00)00195-1.
4. Jacqueline K. Mitchelson, "Seeking the Perfect Balance: Perfectionism and Work-Family Conflict," *Journal of Occupational and Organizational Psychology* 82, no. 2 (June 2009): 349–67, https://doi.org/10.1348/096317908X314874.
5. Jeffrey S. Ashby, Kenneth G. Rice, and James L. Martin, "Perfectionism, Shame, and Depressive Symptoms," *Journal of Counseling & Development* 84, no. 2 (December 2011): 148–56, http://onlinelibrary.wiley.com/doi/10.1002/j.1556-6678.2006.tb00390.x/abstract.
6. James Clear, "Treat Failure Like a Scientist," James Clear (website), https://jamesclear.com/failure-scientist.
7. Kantar and Women Political Leaders, *The Reykjavik Index for Leadership 2019–2020* (London: Kantar, 2019), https://www.womenpoliticalleaders.org/wp-content/uploads/2019/12/The-Reykjavik-Index-Report_DIGITAL-3.pdf.
8. "Maya Angelou Quotes," All Author, accessed November 3, 2020, https://allauthor.com/quotes/88789/.
9. Robert Jones Jr. (@sonofbaldwin), "We can disagree and still love each other unless your disagreement is rooted in my oppression and denial of my humanity and right to exist," Twitter, August 18, 2015, 9:19 a.m., https://twitter.com/SonofBaldwin/status/633644373423562753.

Chapter 7: Taking Small, Daily Action

1. Luis Carretié et al., "Emotion, Attention, and the 'Negativity Bias,' Studied Through Event-Related Potentials," *International Journal of Psychophysiology* 41, no. 1 (May 2001): 75–85, https://doi.org/10.1016/S0167-8760(00)00195-1.
2. Nicole Gugliucci (@NoisyAstronomer), "My friends coined a word: hepeated. For when a woman suggests an idea and it's ignored, but then a guy says same thing and everyone loves it," Twitter, September 22, 2017, 8:01 a.m., https://twitter.com/NoisyAstronomer/status/911213826527436800.

3. Tarana Burke, "History & Inception," me too. (website), accessed November 3, 2020, https://metoomvmt.org/get-to-know-us/history-inception/.
4. Me Too Movement, "About Us," LinkedIn, accessed November 3, 2020, https://www.linkedin.com/company/me-too-movement.
5. Leila Janah, "Why First-World Feminism Just Isn't Enough," GirlBoss, September 25, 2017, https://www.girlboss.com/read/leila-janah-first-world-feminism-essay.
6. Jeanne Shaheen, *Tackling the Gender Gap: What Women Need to Thrive* (US Senate Committee on Small Business & Leadership, 2017), 2, https://www.sbc.senate.gov/public/_cache/files/2/5/25bd7ee9-a37b-4d2b-a91a-8b1ad6f5bd58/536DC6E705BBAD3B555BFA4B60DEA025.sbc-tackling-the-gender-gap.december-2017-final.pdf.
7. Jay Baer, "3 Reasons Word of Mouth Is the Best Way to Grow Your Business," Convince & Convert, https://www.convinceandconvert.com/word-of-mouth/word-of-mouth-best-way-to-grow-your-business/.
8. Andrew McCaskill, "Recommendations from Friends Remain Most Credible Form of Advertising Among Consumers; Branded Websites Are the Second-Highest-Rated Form," Nielsen, September 28, 2015, https://www.nielsen.com/us/en/press-releases/2015/recommendations-from-friends-remain-most-credible-form-of-advertising/.
9. Rosie Murphy, "Local Consumer Review Survey," BrightLocal, December 11, 2019, https://www.brightlocal.com/research/local-consumer-review-survey/.

Chapter 8: Your Voice Matters

1. "Maggie Kuhn," National Women's Hall of Fame, accessed November 3, 2020, https://www.womenofthehall.org/inductee/maggie-kuhn/.
2. Joan Podrazik, "Dr. Brene Brown: Joy Is 'The Most Terrifying, Difficult Emotion' (VIDEO)," HuffPost, March 18, 2013, https://www.huffpost.com/entry/dr-brene-brown-joy-gratitude-oprah_n_2885983.
3. Leslie Shore, "Gal Interrupted, Why Men Interrupt Women and How to Avert This in the Workplace," *Forbes*, January 3, 2017, https://www.forbes.com/sites/womensmedia/2017/01/03/gal-interrupted-why-men-interrupt-women-and-how-to-avert-this-in-the-workplace/#787a7fb517c3.
4. Juliet Eilperin, "White House Women Want to Be in the Room Where It Happens," *Washington Post*, September 13, 2016, https://www.washingtonpost.com/news/powerpost/wp/2016/09/13/white-house-women-are-now-in-the-room-where-it-happens/.
5. Kieran Snyder, "How to Get Ahead as a Woman in Tech: Interrupt Men," Slate, July 23, 2014, https://slate.com/human-interest/2014/07/study-men-interrupt-women-more-in-tech-workplaces-but-high-ranking-women-learn-to-interrupt.html.
6. Colleen Flaherty, "Relying on Women, Not Rewarding Them," Inside Higher

Ed, April 12, 2017, https://www.insidehighered.com/news/2017/04/12/study-finds-female-professors-outperform-men-service-their-possible-professional.

7. Byron Katie (@TheWorkofByronKatie), "A dishonest yes is a no to yourself," Facebook, July 20, 2013, https://www.facebook.com/theworkofbyronkatie/posts/a-dishonest-yes-is-a-no-to-yourself/10151566297234150/.

Chapter 9: Using Your Superpowers for Good

1. Vijay Eswaran, "The Business Case for Diversity in the Workplace is Now Overwhelming," World Economic Forum, April 29, 2019, https://www.weforum.org/agenda/2019/04/business-case-for-diversity-in-the-workplace/.
2. "Loveland Therapy Fund," Loveland Foundation, https://thelovelandfoundation.org/loveland-therapy-fund/.
3. "What We're About," Together Rising, https://togetherrising.org/about/. Glennon Doyle's work has changed my life, particularly her book *Untamed*.
4. "Heifer International," Closing for a Cause, http://www.closingforacause.org/heifer/.
5. Arlan Hamilton (@ArlanWasHere), "Earlier in this interview I was asked if I'd be worried that I was missing "the next Mark Zuckerberg" by not investing in straight white men. Most investors should be asking themselves what if they miss the next tech icon by *only* investing in them," Twitter, August 14, 2019, 12:55 p.m., https://twitter.com/ArlanWasHere/status/1161697904844652544.
6. "What We're About," Together Rising.

Chapter 10: Becoming a Role Model and Making a Lasting Difference

1. Dove, "New Dove Research Finds Beauty Pressures Up, and Women and Girls Calling for Change," PR Newswire, June 21, 2016, https://www.prnewswire.com/news-releases/new-dove-research-finds-beauty-pressures-up-and-women-and-girls-calling-for-change-583743391.html.
2. Lindsay Lowe, "Barbara Walters at 90: Oprah and Other Women Thank Legendary Broadcaster for Paving the Way for Their Careers," *Parade*, September 25, 2019, https://parade.com/928054/lindsaylowe/barbara-walters-inspiring-quotes/.
3. Rachel Thomas et al., *Women in the Workplace*, 5th ed. (Lean In and McKinsey & Company, 2019), 16, https://wiw-report.s3.amazonaws.com/Women_in_the_Workplace_2019.pdf.
4. Rachel Bowley, "A Snapshot of Progress Among Women in the Workforce," *LinkedIn Official Blog*, March 6, 2018, https://blog.linkedin.com/2018/march/6/a-snapshot-of-progress-among-women-in-the-workforce.
5. Kristen Henneman, "Olympian Ruth White Found Freedom in Fencing," USA

Fencing, February 27, 2017, https://www.usafencing.org/news_article/show/762992-olympian-ruth-white-found-freedom-in-fencing.

6. "Ibtihaj Muhammad Biography," Biography, updated April 14, 2019, https://www.biography.com/athlete/ibtihaj-muhammad.
7. Shara Taylor, "The Ibtihaj Effect: Olympic Fencing Medalist's Success Spawns New Generation of Hijab-Wearing Athletes Eager to Thrust and Parry," *New York Daily News*, December 8, 2019, https://www.nydailynews.com/news/national/ny-chelsea-fencing-school-20191208-hiuntkjwqrep3dg26u2y5dzwty-story.html.
8. Sarah Kuta, "Women Who Run for Office Inspire Others to Do the Same, Study Suggests," *Colorado Arts and Sciences Magazine*, July 31, 2018, https://www.colorado.edu/asmagazine/2018/07/31/women-who-run-office-inspire-others-do-same-study-suggests.
9. Brené Brown, *Braving the Wilderness: The Quest for True Belonging and the Courage to Stand Alone* (New York: Random House, 2017), 134.
10. "Aut Scissors Aut Nullus," *LIFE* 51 (January–June 1908): 438, https://books.google.com/books?id=xpYhAQAAMAAJ&q=%22escape+criticism%22#v=snippet&q=%22escape%20criticism%22&f=false.
11. Arlan Hamilton, *It's About Damn Time: How to Turn Being Underestimated into Your Greatest Advantage* (New York: Currency, 2020), 136.
12. Daryl Remley, "5 Inspirational Quotes from Laverne Cox," *The Leader Reader Journal*, February 13, 2020, https://leaderreaderjournal.com/5-inspirational-quotes-from-laverne-cox/.
13. Glennon Doyle, *Untamed* (New York: The Dial Press, 2020), 105.
14. Elizabeth DiAlto, "How to Know Yourself—Why Self-Knowledge Matters for Self-Love," *Embodied* (podcast), August 5, 2020, https://untameyourself.com/340/.
15. Nadia Hallgren, director, *Becoming* (Los Gatos, CA: Higher Grounds Productions and Big Mouth Productions, 2020).

How I Wrote This Book

1. "Creative Nonfiction," Wikipedia, last modified July 30, 2020, https://en.wikipedia.org/wiki/Creative_nonfiction.

Index

F

G

H

I

J

K

L

M

About the Author

Molly Galbraith, CSCS, is the cofounder of Girls Gone Strong (GGS), the world's largest platform providing evidence-based, interdisciplinary health, fitness, nutrition, and pregnancy education for women and the health and fitness professionals who work with them—including industry-leading certification programs and coaching.

The "Strong women lift each other up" philosophy is woven through the fabric of GGS. From employing and educating, to featuring, collaborating with, and investing in women, GGS is dedicated to serving their community of women from 90+ countries around the world.

Molly has spoken all over the world at top conferences and prestigious universities like Yale, and she's been featured in publications like *Time*, *People*, *Today*, ABC, and *Women's Health*.

She lives with her life and business partner, Casey.

GirlsGoneStrong.com

MollyGalbraith.com